The Ultimate Broadway Musical List Book

The Ultimate *Broadway Musical* List Book

Steven M. Friedman

The Ultimate Broadway Musical List Book

iUniverse books may be ordered through booksellers or by contacting:

iUniverse
1663 Liberty Drive
Bloomington, IN 47403
www.iuniverse.com
1-800-Authors (1-800-288-4677)

ISBN: 978-1-4917-8695-6 (sc)
ISBN: 978-1-4917-8696-3 (e)

Library of Congress Control Number: 2016901972

Print information available on the last page.

iUniverse rev. date: 2/16/2016

Contents

How Did This Happen?

While enjoying my newfound past time, lecturing on the topic of Broadway Musical History at sea, I met an insightful, charismatic, truly brilliant man by the name of Shelby Coffey III. He loved my lectures and based upon his background and insight from his positions at the Washington Post, CNN, The LA Times and The Newseum I asked him a fateful question.

"How do I write a book and pull what I do together in a format that could be interesting?"

He very quickly responded—"People like lists"—tell people how you got your passion, write your lists and then explain them.

It was magic—there it was and here it is.

I don't think this is ever meant to be serious, but I hope it can create lots of fun conversation among musical theatre aficionados. So Shelby, I thank you for the terrific inspiration,

Before the Lists, Passions Got Started

Maybe I was 7 or 8. I am not quite sure, but I recall vividly taking an original cast recording of "Can-Can" "Guys and Dolls", "My Fair Lady", or " The Music Man" and putting it standing up on the inside lid of my Victrola and listening to great music and imaging what the play must have been like that the music came from. I remember Lilo singing "I Love Paris" and Hans Conreid singing "Never be an Artist". Forget that I could barely understand the story or did not even care yet who Cole Porter was. This was a magical way to spend my time listening to great Broadway albums of a special era that were hanging around the house. Who knew that these great moments would create a passion so strong, it lasted for the rest of my life.

My very real favorite of course was "My Fair Lady". The chords of the overture, sounding so much more elegant than anything else, the lithe tune that follows "I Have Often Walked Down This Street Before" or Rex Harrison singing a "Why Can't a Woman Be More Like a Man?" I knew every lyric to every single song and could imagine what it must have been like to sit in the theatre and see the plays.

In 1957, I can clearly recall watching the Sunday night production of "Cinderella" with Julie Andrews and when my birthday occurred a few weeks later my father bringing me home the recorded album. I too sat in my own little corner and played the music over and over again just filling me with energy recalling the great TV event of a few weeks earlier.

These recordings became my special time.

Passions just happen sometime. As the Sixties advanced there were more and more records. "Camelot" became a favorite; oh, they might burn Guinevere at the stake? How cool was that!

But my luckiest moment came when a friend's parent asked if I would like to see "Bye Bye Birdie" at the National Theatre at an upcoming Saturday matinee here in Washington DC. I was about 11 at the time and was not quite sure what this musical was about, somehow the recording had not infiltrated my house yet.

It was amazing. I recall the fourth row seats. The magic as teenagers were hanging from boxes singing about Hugo and Kim getting pinned, learning about Conrad Birdie and I was carried away to Sweet Apple Ohio. No words can describe the exhilaration and enthusiasm I was feeling watching and recalling this event. I just recall it vividly! I was so unfamiliar with real theatre we didn't quite understand that when the lights came up there was more to come. We thought maybe it was over but no one left.

With the Album at my house, after I saved my allowance (I think it was a $5.00 album) I began to choreograph and re-create all of the moments in "Bye Bye Birdie" for my family and the poor relatives that had to sit through my entire 45 minute rendition playing every character in the script. But I was hooked.

Luckily there was a summer theatre nearby, called Shady Grove Music Fair and it was a part of the circuit owned by Guber and Gross (Barbara Walters was married to Lee Guber). This venue under a tent initially was where I was introduced to even more Broadway than you can imagine. George Gobel (remember him) played Albert in Bye Bye Birdie, Patrice Munsel played Can-Can, Jayne Mansfield played Lorelei Lee in "Gentleman Prefer Blondes"(I even have her autograph) Martha Raye played Sally Adams in "Call Me Madam" and for you trivia people imagine Gail Storm In Finnian's Rainbow. (I'm sorry if you don't know who Gail Storm is).

This summer stock circuit introduced me to the great musicals of the time and I was so enthralled that at school all of the non-jock kids would talk about the musicals. Oh. By the way I was a non-jock kid. One of my friends at the time Mark Freedman was a willing conversationalist as his father ran the PR for the Shady Grove Theater and we would sit and devour every last detail of the shows for months on end.

By the time I was 12 or 13 if a good musical came to town I got a 1.99 second balcony seat and was able to ride the bus to downtown DC to the National Theatre to see something fantastic.

1964 really hit pay dirt for me!

I went to Detroit every summer to visit my grandmother and her family of 4 overly interfering sisters who themselves belonged in Billy Crystals "700 Sundays."

In any event I was invited to a big event. There was a new "Mostel" show at the Fisher Theatre. Would I like to go? I jumped at it, knew nothing about what we were going to see, and sort of thought I had heard of Zero Mostel somehow. That it was a musical called "Fiddler on the Roof" and it was on its way to New York with an intermediate stop in Washington DC was greater than cool. The Fisher had just re-opened and it was like no other theater I had ever seen. It was huge, lush, exciting. The National was dull old and small.

I got the program and learned that this story is based upon Shalom Aleichem short stories and I had a sort of a picture he was a Russian writer who wrote Jewish stories. That was about all I knew. My grandmother who was a very modern non accent speaking first generation person was skeptical of the whole evening. I frankly did not catch at my age of 13 that she was in fact from Poland and had come from there at a young age and would have a connection to the proceedings. All I knew was I was in for a great musical adventure. A Broadway tryout!

So all dressed up in a suit and tie (that was the required dress in those days) off to the theatre!

The lights went down and the stage did not have a curtain in front of it as I recall. There was a little house and a fiddler was sitting atop the house playing some music. Suddenly this man (Zero Mostel) came out on stage and pointed to a fiddler on his roof and went on from there. Suddenly the entire cast of town's people town came out singing this song about which they were and what they were about. Tradition! They kept singing and I suddenly figured out that this was about a Jewish community, and since this was about 4 months after my Bar Mitzvah I was getting a very deep connection to this. I did not know there were Jewish musicals. (Actually there hadn't been.)

After the daughters sang "Matchmaker, Matchmaker " I also had another thought as my grandmother could not get married until her older sister was married first and that caused all sorts of family complications including my grandmother and grandfather eloping. I was watching a story that related to my family.

Then it was Sabbath prayer and a scrim covered the entire stage with families all over town lighting Sabbath candles and suddenly I had tears rolling down my cheek, I did not know Jewish musicals could sing about Sabbath. It went on from there. I was truly emotional as the wedding pogrom ruined a wonderful occasion and then later as the whole town is sent away because they were Jewish.

In the back of my mind I knew that is how we all ended up in America, but I didn't know musicals sang about these things. When the lights came up my grandmother and two of my aunts then had a great deal of discussion how the rabbi was being portrayed as a schlemiel, and that the characters troubled them and they kept saying it wasn't really like that. They in fact were a bit insulted by what they thought were troubling stereotypical portrayals.

I couldn't figure out what it wasn't really like. I just loved all 3 hours and 45 minutes of it. It was long. The program already had songs being cut out and new songs appeared that were not in the program. I do remember vividly the dream sequence, and "To Life" in the bar as well as the final chords after "Anatevka." All I knew was I felt like an insider and had seen something really special.

Upon returning home to DC, I told everyone. There is this new musical coming to the National and it's Jewish and we have to go again. People thought I was being a bit over zealous about it even for me, but I pestered everyone I could find. My parents and all of their friends went. They all came home impressed.

I was developing a huge personal dilemma. My most recent acquisition was the Carol Channing "Hello Dolly" Album which in 1964 was the previous Washington DC big deal as it had played here on Broadway tryout only months earlier. How could I suddenly give that album up along with "Camelot" for "Fiddler on the Roof?"

Somehow poor Jerry Herman was taking a second place to Bock and Harnick. I did give Leonard Bernstein and Stephen Sondheim some listens (West Side Story) and of course I had been attached to my Ethel Merman "Gypsy" album. But this "Fiddler on the Roof" was new, and totally connected to me and not just some new random musical. I just listened to it over and over and over.

By now I was in ninth grade and had discovered that I did have a voice that with some training might get me somewhere. I was a classical piano student and was learning Rachmaninoff and Shubert at the time so learning to sing correctly seemed a whole lot easier. It did not take two hands co-ordination and counting.

As I studied and learned to use my voice correctly my love for theatre grew. One illicit issue was that my piano teacher was very old school and she only believed in classical music. I had just discovered vocal selection books and I had to hide them in the piano bench whenever she was at the house for my lesson. Yet, as ninth grade took me to high school my singing skills kept getting better and better and my piano skills kept getting pushed aside.

My theater trivia knowledge of the time was growing. I read the "New York Times" theater section weekly, and knew who was opening in what, remember the review of Chita Rivera in "Bajour", or the Julie Harris Skyscraper (do you remember those?) Plus the list of long running Broadway shows that appeared every Sunday. Best were the Hirschfeld cartoons of the opening play that week and looking for the Nina's to appear in the lines drawings.

Now ask me who played on the local Redskin team I was clueless.

In the tenth grade, now becoming a burgeoning Broadway expert in my own mind, there was this odd flop of a show that my high school decided to tackle "On A Clear Day You Can See Forever". It had this glorious score, but a book that just made little sense, about a woman who gets hypnotized to stop smoking and through hypnosis discovers she lived a previous life and has ESP. I was cast as a character that had an affair with the main character in a previous life and sang the beautiful ballad "She Wasn't You". It made little sense and I was a bit annoyed that my high school debut was to be encased in a play that closed without a real run, but I do recall making people get excited when I sang.

It's amazing who a high school can produce. A "senior" was very talented was made assistant to the director. Her name was Elodie Keene and later in life became a director of many hit series on television. Obviously her helping me did not help me become less wooden, but she was adamant that my rendition of "She Wasn't You" was a major part of the musical and wooden or not my singing voice was incredible and at 16 I got my first grown up part. So to this day I owe Elodie my future, where ever she may be! Without her I may never have gone further.

I was becoming possessed by Broadway ambitions and thought maybe I can really do something with this. I really had a fine voice that was growing in maturity and nuance and frankly when given the chance could blast the walls apart. I had to learn how to control that, but my voice was huge.

The next year I got to have a one scene part singing in Saroyan's "The Time of Your Life"—(who was he anyway?), and had seen a recent summer production of Dorothy Lamour in "Pal Joey" I recalled the lyric form "Zip " in "Pal Joey"—"will Saroyan ever write a great play." Being in one I wasn't sure.

By now being a junior in High School I was a hot ticket top notch baritone in my own mind at least. I was studying with a student of Todd Duncan (the original Porgy), could do a tear rendering version of "Edelweiss" and if asked to do a barn raising "Impossible Dream". I was always being asked to sing, everywhere. It was very heady and as a teenager you almost become snobby about it.

One odd summer evening in 1967 I went on a blind date. I was told we would have tons in common. She loved to sing, was a great dancer (a requirement for all blind dates at the time) and liked Broadway musicals. Well, upon meeting

Brenda, it was love at first sight so they say. We had such strong mutual connections with the music that we shortly thereafter became an item. We went to the theater all of the time and sang songs together at the piano.

She went to the competing high school and their plays had gargantuan scenery and so forth and my high school took the minimalist approach. Her high school launched Goldie Hawn and Connie Chung and Sylvester Stallone, my school launched doctors and lawyers LOL.

"How to Succeed in Business" had become a favorite of mine since seeing with it camp friend Jimmy Bortz, and her high school was doing it, It was to open and run two weekends in April. Sadly the weekend it was to open Martin Luther King Jr. was shot and riots broke out in Washington and the play had to be cancelled for respect, fear and safety.

By this point in time I was able to see a production of the touring Company of "Cabaret"—I must sadly admit that I did not get it in the least. Why was there an all-girl band? Why was it not until the second act it got serious, I was really baffled by the evening. I was forming opinions though and just could not get my head around it. Masterpieces take time to accept sometimes.

By then I got to be a part of "West Side Story". It a long story but let's just say I got to exercise my pipes a bit and kill Tony at the end.

My pipes were really taking on strength and power and the rivals (the music and theater depts.) decided to perform a Gilbert and Sullivan operetta "The Sorcerer". I was doing what I did best play the male ingénue! I played young Alexis Poindexter and sang my heart out.

Performing was to become a passion. I ate slept and drank what my next part would be. At 17 you are truly getting into this or you don't. It was really my thing.

With the Vietnam War brewing and the draft becoming

such an issue I was securing my future. My voice teacher had been a Singing Sergeant and I was convinced that if I had to get drafted one day I would do it singing. The good news was that never had to happen.

By the time senior year came around Brenda and I were really " theatre people" Our friend Susan Hoffman who was working in the periphery of the theater locally knew lots of people and talked with us about them often. We saw everything we could and she talked to us about theatre adventures. We all had our moments in the sun. I played another male ingénue in "Once Upon A Mattress" and Brenda played Fanny Brice's mother at her school. But now I had a real chance to do something.

I auditioned for the Music Fair Circuit. My esteemed theatre teacher Pat Dalla-Santa from Bethesda Chevy Chase High School was one of several judges. This was also the summer theatre that gave Goldie Hawn her start. This was a very big deal. I had never done a professional audition before and was really nervous. I was called in and to tell you the truth don't even recall what it was I sang. All I know was I was being sent to New York for the call backs. I almost passed out.

My parents took a professional approach. They said go but you pay for your own trip and expenses. The Eastern Air Shuttle to New York was $18.00 and my room at the Wellington Hotel was $9.00. I don't even recall where the audition was but I sort of recall the place. It was upstairs at a dingy room. Thirty guys stood in a circle around the director table and we revolved one by one singing sixteen bars.

Again I didn't have a clue what I sang, but do recall hearing to the 20 or so before me" thank you ", next one up "thank you", next one up " thank you" . Sobs broke out and more thank you. Once in a while you would hear take a seat. That happened to me. After another round of 16 more bars, I was told that I should wait a bit longer. My heart was thumping. They then matched men and women. I was told shortly thereafter that I would be an alternate for" Mame" that would tour that summer with Edie Adams. No alternate needs ever occurred, and that alternate situation lasted for about 18 hours. What a relief. I really wanted to go off to Michigan State and frankly figured out quickly that I did not want to spend my life in a circle singing 16 bars and be that dependent on it. I thought about it a lot. I did not think I wanted to be a performer for a living.

In my second year at Michigan State I got involved with a group of kids who all loved theatre. We had this wild idea that for 99 cents we could do a show and travel the dorm complexes. The Sondheim Musical "Company" had opened and all of us in the know were playing it nonstop and wanting to sing everything Sondheim. He suddenly had become the master of our musical lives.

By this point in time I was studying with the head of the voice department at MSU not as a voice major but he felt that my instrument was up for his astute coaching. I agreed and suddenly the baritone voice was reaching tenor strata. I was adding a note a semester and luckily not losing any of the low notes that baritones cherish. It was pretty quick to determine that I had a tenor lyric quality and that it possessed a baritone richness that tenors often lacked.

In the meantime with the fledgling theatre group we did lots of musicals. I was somewhat the ringleader expert as I had seen so many, had been to London and seen productions, and helped spearhead a group of no drama student theater lovers.

There were many there who we enjoyed and got to meet. Peter Marinos who was way more talented than any of us and went on to be in the best Broadway could provide for 35 years and even worked on his chops with us. Peter had an antic driven style that could be gracious winning and just over the top inspiring. I was always thrilled that this really super talented guy thought hanging with us was OK.

So during this time period I was able to have access to some terrific roles. I played Joe Hardy in "Damn Yankees", and loved it. I played El Gallo, in "The Fantasticks" with a case of measles interrupting my rehearsals. The night the play opened I stood at the back of theatre waiting to make my entrance and my first lyric was try to remember—I went blank and said to the stage manager (my wife) try to remember, try to remember what and then the lights came up and the lyrics were right there after all. As much as I loved to perform, I never ever forgot the fright of that moment.

I was learning pretty quickly that the idea of performing was a lot more fun than performing. I was developing a strong hatred of temperamental rehearsal time.

That summer we travelled to New England and my friend Peter was performing in Summer Stock there and I kept thinking I know someone who is going to really make it. I took comfort in knowing that making it with my voice had less and less interest for me. Being married at twenty also changed my ideas about that as well.

The USO had come to Michigan State to cast a travel show to Europe for 6 weeks, although not a theatre major the head of the theater department mentioned to me that I was perfect for the cast he was assembling. What a great opportunity it would be for me to travel that way and have the benefit of building my skill set performing at that level. I was excited but there was a problem .I could not take my wife with me. I was taken aback; can't she do props or something?

The answer was no and I decided that a USO tour was not my goal under those conditions.

Time went on and I truly kept my voice in shape. I did a lot of choir singing and solo work over time but the desire to truly perform grew less and less. I found out that I just hated rehearsals. I hated temperamental overly fussy directors who were stupid. I hated people's tantrums. I hated people being late.

For the next number of years I just studied learned music and added notes to my range.

In 1987 and 1988 I had been living in a small community outside of Boston and did two incredible concerts with a fellow tenor and performer Robbie Solomon. He was the cantor and music director in Sharon, MA. We did these two wonderful evenings of classical and theatre music. I was a nervous wreck because I was putting myself out there as a truly accomplished singer and I thought I must have been crazy or something but our event raised good money for the community and it was a real thrill to do these. My tenor voice was really reaching all of the high notes and singing Mahler, and Schumann not to mention even an aria or two. People came and that was astonishing for me. It was something that I'm still very proud of as it was good work for someone that was not singing professionally.

I had a great teacher in Boston at the time, Bruce Kolb, who gave me great advice. I was really nervous about these performances and he said something to the effect of that if anyone else was talented enough to take my place on stage and do what I was doing I should let them. I never forgot that as it did put the nerves into place.

Moving ahead a bit, In 1996 we had an event. It was our 25th wedding anniversary.

My wife and I performed often together over years, auctioning ourselves off as waiters and waitress who cooked dinner and then sang (and donated the proceeds to charities). As we were all performers at this point in time, we 4 Friedman's performed together and did a concert for 200 people. The boys also talented, and nationally recognized performers at that time, agreed of course, but they grumbled and groaned and just did not have the vision of how unique this was. No one ever knew a family that could do this. We were really proud of it and still to this day think it was a very special moment.

We did all show music and Brenda and I started with "Sing" from "A Chorus Line". We did great music but since it was our 25th we included "Do You Love Me" from "Fiddler". It had a key line—after all 25 years was a key component of that song. I never could get through it dry eyed on a rehearsal nor could I do it then. To me it is one of our true family milestones.

I continued to sing publicly until about 1999. I was so annoyed at rehearsing that the public singing was not worth the bother.

My son Darrin got married in 2000, and it came with the entry of a coloratura into the family. Well every family needs another female voice! Heather was fantastic. The direction came down that we were hosting a rehearsal dinner where all of the kids friends, the kids and we would do a cabaret evening of wedding related favorites. I sang "You are Love" from "Showboat" and was the third voice in "Getting Married today" from "Company". Well here we were again the von Friedman family singers at large.

That was the last public singing that my wife ever did and that really is sad for me to think about as we really did fun things together.

However, she came out of brief retirement in 2001.

My family gave me a gift. They offered me a recording as a gift in a studio, with real equipment. It took a year to pull off but the duets with my kids, doing "Maria" and "Tonight" from "West Side Story", the duets form "The Fantasticks" still soar to me every time I listen to them. It is a very special thing to hear and it's pretty darn good. My favorite moment was doing "Officer Krupuke" with my boys, not even able to keep it straight and having a great time doing it. Tough when all three of us sound similarly alike!

All the while not performing in public I kept studying. I had a terrific teacher at this point Joan Benner Kaplon. She had been a Metropolitan Opera diva in training and events brought her to DC. She is and was fantastic. I was crazy about her method and style and she got me ready for that recording. I even did "Maria" in the original high key thanks to her. She was always on my case that I didn't sing enough but I could just not find the project that made it seem important.

My consulting practice kept me up in front of people so I guess I was performing all the time, just differently.

I also fulfilled my theater itch by becoming a part of the board of the now Tony award winning Signature Theatre in Arlington, Virginia. I learned a lot about non-profit theatre. It has to be run like a business. The artistic director Eric Schaeffer is truly a genius and can re-invent musicals like no one's business. Yet pressure to create revenue in the young theatre was a challenge. When you are on an arts board it is all about give and get. The board was transitioning and it just did not understand the role they had in that arena. I also hate board politics and had decided that when I accepted to do this I would enjoy the theatre connection and the inside knowledge it would be fun to have. It gave access to many exciting events and people.

I chaired a fundraiser concert for the theatre enjoyed working with Eric on that project. Yet the politics were truly overwhelming. Money was challenging and I was always so frustrated that the board did not do more to raise funds aggressively. Building a new theatre was at hand and it was complicated and burdensome. It was not a good fit as my board experiences truly had me at odds with the direction this group was going. We all have to move on sometimes!

So now fast forward to 2011.

Brenda and I had been on numerous cruises over the years to all sorts of places in the world. In fact we were lucky to think we had been so lucky to have been so many places. On several cruises there were speakers who had claimed to have really interesting show biz topics. One lecture series was to be from a guy who had been a Hollywood editor talking about all sorts of Hollywood lore. He was awful and his facts all wrong and it was disappointing. When he put up a picture of Rita Hayworth and said it was Betty Grable I left the lecture.

After another cruise with an awful speaker, I could not believe these people got on cruise ships to lecture. Doing some real research I figured out the process. It was not an easy one either. I went through the hoops and figured well it's a cute idea and it will never happen. It involved that I create a syllabus and knowing that I can sing, I envisioned a sort of three dimensional lecture series.

From that I created a history of Broadway Musical Theatre using the decade approach and looked for music that could translate to give examples of the times that I could sing. Then bang one day the agent called me and said we have a Baltic Cruise would you like to be on it. I just never dreamt that this was going to happen as I thought it might be a crazy idea but who would ever ask me!

Before I went they asked me to do another cruise as well. Again I found this hard to believe. Yet, as I was developing this lecture series at local community senior centers the lectures were becoming extremely popular. I was being called and sought after more and more. So suddenly the voice I trained all of these years and some acquired knowledge was being used to my own personal enjoyment as well.

So now to the lists! I love lists because we all argue with them. We might agree but we might also disagree. 10 best lists always create fun and lively discussion. So researching my passion, here are my lists. These are lists of Broadway musicals dissected in a lot of ways. Different musicals come on different lists. That is the duplication that sometimes will occur in the discussion. The same musical may be on more than one list. So forgive the repetition that may occur.

I also found out as I researched that there were some amazing facts out there I never knew, such as Judy Dench was to be the original Grizabella in "Cats". Who knew!

Keep notes and see what you agree and disagree with.

12 Best Musicals from 1927-1949

This is an odd historical list as it spans almost 22 years. It was an era of great musical composition that hit the pop-charts and is now referred to as "The American Songbook". The era had lots of exciting music created for a lot of Broadway musicals that over time have not aged well, however looking at the time period from "Showboat" to "South Pacific" as an evolutionary time can justify the list.

The greats were the composers, Kern, Gershwin, Rodgers and Hart, Cole Porter to name just a few. The music that these gave us is often the beloved standards we cherish.

- ☆ *Showboat*
- ☆ *Of Thee I Sing*
- ☆ *Anything Goes*
- ☆ *Porgy and Bess*
- ☆ *Lady In The Dark*
- ☆ *Pal Joey*
- ☆ *Oklahoma!*
- ☆ *On The Town*
- ☆ *Carousel*
- ☆ *Annie Get Your Gun*
- ☆ *Kiss Me Kate*
- ☆ *South Pacific*

Showboat

The musical /operetta style that created the foundation for the modern musical is truly exceptional and present in

"Showboat". The music was still written in a semi-operatic style with a recitative that came first before the song gets sung and the overall sweeping approach was operatic in tone but yet accessible in a broad main stream way potentially.

Jerome Kern and Oscar Hammerstein II reacted to the Edna Ferber novel as a unique idea for a musical. It had a sprawling fifty year story line, an interracial story line, a focus on gambling addiction, and the development of a career, and the costs it can create in ones' life. This was in 1927! No one had ever seen a musical that had serious content in it like this before and it was so exciting that Florenz Ziegfeld even produced it. Helen Morgan, a major star of the time took the role of Julie, the mixed race singer on the Showboat.

"Showboat" is seen even today as challenging as it requires a cast that is large and has to be multi-racial. It also has challenges in the way it is written. There are many versions of "Showboat" as over time there has been the attempt to soften the African American dialogue that in today's world is not politically correct. It was written with a great deal of research at the time, yet it is not comfortable for today's ears sadly.

Further, several "Showboat" scripts had been used over the years including several film treatments. The first in 1929, when sound was young did not give the movie its true breadth of spoken scenarios. The 1936 version directed by James Whale is the most accurate to the original stage version but it is in black and white and has been hidden for years as MGM who later secured the property wanted to make sure the original film as done by a competitive studio was long forgotten.

However the MGM version is not a film of the entire Showboat as written. Interestingly Lena Horne was originally cast in the role of Julie, the singer on the Showboat who has interracial parents. This is a focus of the story. She was very outspoken about racial prejudice and was involved with the

NAACP. MGM invented a shade of make up for her called "Light Egyptian", she recorded the songs on the lot only to be substituted by Ava Gardner, and dubbed by Lena Horne. She was considered too risky suddenly and taken off the film.

Paul Robeson who sang Ol' Man River also has added his share of controversy to the history of 'Showboat.' He sang "Ol' Man River" around the world in the 1930's with his robust bass voice and even went to Russia as the most famous African American singer in the world. He felt that Communism did not consider race as a barrier and naively believed this was a good system of government. He was not aware of the many prejudices the Communist regime had until after WWII when Jewish friends and others had disappeared. He too was blacklisted and he retreated from Public career view.

"Showboat" has been revised over the years often as it is theatrically popular and its score is glorious and magnificent and still widely sung today.

Hal Prince created an outstanding revival in 1996 that took many published versions of "Showboat" and recreated these for a version suitable for today. It is an outstanding example of how a great musical with many versions can remain relevant at close to being a 90 year old piece of work.

~

Of Thee I Sing!

The Gershwin's were writing great musicals in the era and were struggling to be taken seriously if that was possible for a team writing popular musicals. The idea of a satire of the Presidential election system seemed at first to be a strange musical topic, but with a book by Kaufmann and Ryskind the musical took shape.

The basic idea is that a presidential candidate will run on a love ticket and kiss the same woman in all 48 states. Scandal breaks out when an opposing political rival creates a story that he is having an affair at the same time and has walked away from the beauty queen who claims his affection.

"Of Thee I Sing" is clever and witty, and still resonates today mocking the Vice President and the Supreme Court in satirical fashion and due to its strong farcical content garnered a Pulitzer Prize the first time ever for a Musical.

~

Anything Goes

There was great competition among the tune smiths of the time. Between Hollywood calling for musicals and the stage options the major composers of the day were very busy. Cole Porter was certainly among that group.

He had looked at the idea of a musical aboard a luxury liner with Bolton and Woodehouse writing the book. A sinking of a ship seemed to derail the project yet was revised and reenergized with a stellar cast including Ethel Merman.

The story is a bit inane and typical of the time. A young stock broker sees a woman who is to marry an Englishman and thus sets sail for England stowing away on her ship. In the meantime as he steals away he finds his friend nightclub singer turned evangelist Reno Sweeney to be onboard. The story is a typical 1930's musical filled with ridiculous antics but features the great Cole Porter score including "You're the top", "I Get a Kick out of You" and of course the title song.

Over the decades as revivals occurred more and more Cole Porter hits were added from other shows including 'Friendship" and "Delovely"

Over time 'Anything Goes" is considered the typical musical of the era and one of the most successful at the time.

~

Porgy and Bess

Dubose Hayword had written a play based upon the novel "Porgy" and George Gershwin fell in love with the idea of setting it to music with his brother Ira. He felt the story deserved a very deep and tuneful setting and researched the southern black music of the time and decided his musical style for "Porgy and Bess" would be based upon the folk song style he heard and as a result named the piece a folk opera.

Truthfully the musicals of the time being light and fluffy entertainments did not make good comparison to the deeply integrated musical style that "Porgy and Bess" set forth. The evolution of the characters totally set to music was far too different for the tastes of the time.

The cast featured a cast of classically trained African American singers which was a daring artistic choice at the time. Porgy is a disabled black beggar living in the slums of Charleston and deals with his attempts to save an addicted Bess from her abusive partner and drug dealer.

The opera startled audiences in that it was almost totally sung, had sweeping musical passages and was in fact very dark story telling for the time. There were no tap dances or light comic scenes.

The opera was performed in a musical theatre house where black audiences were not even welcome to see the performance.

This disturbed Todd Duncan and Anne Brown (the original Porgy and Bess greatly). In fact over time Todd Duncan refused to perform the role if integrated audiences were not allowed to see it performed. Upon opening the "NY Times" was not clear what they had witnessed. It did not receive rave reviews at all and was almost accepted with a great indifference. The reviews were almost condescending suggesting that The Gershwin's were too lofty in their ambitions. In fact the style was even referred to as drudgery for the average theatre goer.

"Porgy and Bess" only ran for a short time in its original run and the effort although it toured was laden by the lack of positive critical reception.

After the death of George Gershwin, "Porgy and Bess" received a major revival in the mid 1940's again with Todd Duncan reprising his role of Porgy. Yet the cast would not perform in any segregated theatre.

Mr. Duncan who was a masterful classical Baritone retreated to Washington DC and taught voice and music at Howard University. (A note, my first three voice teachers were all students of Todd Duncan here in Washington, DC). They taught his methods and vocal strategies. As a result I always felt as if I were a great-grandchild of Gershwin. No it doesn't make sense but it's my vision of my learning.

"Porgy and Bess" has been a challenged work ever since. There have been revivals over the years and many were successful but they were all regarded as museum viewings of an artistically challenged work. There was a mediocre movie made in the 1950's and it was not helping the work gain stature in the least. It took until the early 1970's for the Houston Opera to mount what has been labeled the most successful version of "Porgy and Bess". It toured nationally and was a celebration of the master work that "Porgy and Bess" has become. In addition this production was filmed for television.

In recent years the American Repertory Theater in Boston revisited "Porgy and Bess". To rethink the scale and libretto into a more manageable form the vision of what Porgy and Bess once was to a less complex work—still with its music in tact but in many places revised. The most highbrow of critics did not agree with the approach. In fact a famous letter to the "NY Times" from Stephen Sondheim, blasted all involved for watering down a masterpiece. Audra MacDonald and Norm Lewis were acclaimed for their portrayals and the revival did receive a Tony for Best Revival, but it is still a controversial position among the purists. To them this is not the "Porgy and Bess" that was initially imagined.

~

Lady in the Dark

Many of the musicals on the 1940's had sex as a theme yet no one shouted it out loud from the rafters. Yet the subject was there in full view as was demonstrated in what would today be considered PG-13 fashion.

The first of many requests, to Ira Gershwin to work with musical composition, Ira Gershwin responded to the request from Kurt Weill to write a musical based upon the emerging field of psychoanalysis. They chose a character in the world of high fashion to be in the tumultuous throws of emotional chaos due to conflicting love affairs that she was having. These affairs took a woman who was determined and focused into someone who could get nothing done.

It's hard to believe in those days that a musical, in very simple retrospect, is not much more than who a woman which of three men that she is swooning over, could cause such a sensation. To think this character is living with a married man who will not divorce his wife, and cannot figure out the one man she really loves as the basis of the plot seems trivial today. Psychanalysis is helping her figure it all out. Sensitivities change over time, yet this question plagued the leading lady and it thus became our concern too.

The "ravishing" Gertrude Lawrence was chosen to play the editor of a major fashion magazine who herself was a diva of enormous proportions. She was praised for her ability to not over act or over emote in her style but truly act a part that was tailor made for her. As Brooks Atkinson noted at the time "...Gertrude Lawrence she is a goddess: that's all."

Moss Hart who directed, imagined Lisa Elliot (the lead character) directing a musical "circus" decided that the musical numbers would come alive as she underwent her analysis. This was a breakthrough in musical theatre story telling. This was considered modern and very contemporary. The use of large turntables which was a new staging technology at the time set everything in motion. This enabled a story to move in ways that musical theater had yet to be accustomed.

In addition to a great comic turn, a newcomer by the name of Danny Kaye had a supporting role singing what would become a trademark, the tongue twisting "Tchaikovsky", a song of numerous Russian names in rapid fire timing.

As we look back on this, and this was a major hit at the time, it is a little odd to think that the likes of an Miranda Priestly in the 1940's could have been sent to therapy over a bunch of guys, but then again that was the time and going to see a shrink was so new that "Lady In the Dark" pushed the envelope. It was a huge success for everyone involved and created theatre magic at the time.

If you have real curiosity about this you can go to YOUTUBE and search Julie Andrews singing "The Saga of Jenny" from the movie "STAR" based upon Gertrude Lawrence. It features a great moment from "Lady in the Dark" being sung by Julie as Gertrude. There was also a movie made with Ginger Rogers that left most of the music out.

~

Pal Joey

The John O' hara stories about a hoofer in Depression era Chicago form the basis for the musical he penned with Rogers and Hart. This was not the most positively received of their work but even with mixed reviews ran for a healthy period of time based upon their previous works.

Again it is the morality of the times that plagued the success of "Pal Joey". This was not your typical love story by any means and again trying to break through barriers in musical story telling the sexual innuendos and relationships as they were presented offended audiences and left them cold.

The story of a callous guy who romances multiple women at the same time as well as being "kept" by an older woman frankly startled the prudish audience. It is not to say that Joey as a lead character is anything to be considered as charming but in today's world the lyrics and the story would never have offended the masses as "Pal Joey" did in 1940.

The character of Joey was so not typical of the time that many encouraged the songwriting duo to give up the project. It just did not seem to be a story for the bright and brassy musical stage of the era.

The critical forces were truly divided. The lyrics to "Bewitched, Bothered and Bewildered" were considered so tasteless that the song had several versions and cut the sauciest lyrics.

It took 11 years to finally see "Pal Joey" as a respected hit. Jule Styne among others produced it in a 1952 revival as times had changed in the 11 years since its opening. It was still the same characters and the same plot, but people had grown up now and they could accept more odious adult material as fodder for Broadway musical theatre.

Oklahoma

The play "Green Grow the Lilacs " was a play from the early 1930's that the Theatre Guild felt would be ripe for musicalization. Rodgers and Hart had examined the piece, but Hart thought writing about yokels on the country was far from the urbane style he enjoyed writing in. He was also consumed by his alcoholism and needed a break.

Hammerstein had looked at the material as well and Jerome Kern also felt it was just not interesting enough to become something that he wanted to become involved with. This then created a new partnership opportunity. Rodgers and Hammerstein were approached separately and then suggested to each other. Rodgers was struggling with a challenged writing relationship with Lorenz Hart, and Hammerstein himself was in a career trough thinking that his style of writing was not widely sought after in the early 1940's.

It was grand thinking and although a seemingly simple story about a cowboy in Oklahoma who falls in love with a farmer's daughter and their friends. It hid a far deeper subtext of sexual awakening in the context of the Oklahoma territory becoming a state. Yes we've all seen it and if you look at the simplistic basis of the story it could be said its' about who is going to take someone to a picnic. Yet in its layers it is far more.

The ambitious changes of the Broadway musical story telling represented in "Showboat" re-emerged here. Each song was a strong presentation of the characters thoughts and feeling.

The plot of "Oklahoma" is not really the point but it is the different approaches that "Oklahoma!" uses that set this so apart. First in contrast to the musicals of the time, the curtain rises on a character sitting on her porch churning butter while off stage you hear the opening strains of 'Oh

What A Beautiful Mornin". It was unusual to not have an opening chorus number and to have a character start to establish themselves through the lyrics they were singing.

Further the device of a love song that is like a conversation and not just a love song was truly unique in "People Will Say We're in Love". The richness of the characterization through lyrics in song was unlike the past where any song might do for a character and this new approach tied every word back to deep characterization. You learned of Curly's optimism, Laurie's sly immature, yet coquettish manner, Ado Annie's' coming of age and Will Parkers naiveté all in song. Yes the dialogue supports their actions but the lyrics in the songs further enhance their characters.

As Hammerstein was writing the lyrics first before setting them to music this enabled the team to write fluidly as if the lyrics were still a part of the dialogue of the script. This was seamless. This was also not the usual style in which Hammerstein had worked in his prior relationship with Kern.

After all "I'm Just a Girl Who Cain't Say no" is about someone knowing that women should be enjoying their sexuality. The words are a dialogue of justification for Ado Annie. She wanted to be a grown up woman and was still being dominated by mores and childhood behaviors.

Also the darkness of a character that collects pornography and had a dark past that may have involved murder is additional plot detail that was unlike any other musical before it.

Rodgers and Hammerstein envisioned a play cast with unknowns and built careers for several out of the originality of the musical. The themes and motifs connect each character throughout the entire story and the skills of the acting team catapulted Oklahoma! to its success.

Agnes DeMille of course created dance sequences that told the story in way that dance had never been used before in musical theatre. She created a "Dream Ballet" that told the entire story to dance, literally shifting the previously used idea of dance routines into choreography.

Without "Oklahoma" there could be nothing else that we've seen since. To say "I've seen Oklahoma a million times is a shame" It needs to be seen and examined from an adult coming of age perspective and understanding the roots of its drama.

~

On The Town

The age of innocence interrupted by war!

Jerome Robbins had created a ballet entitled "Fancy Free" that was set to the music of Leonard Bernstein. While impressed with the ballet and it initial reception the idea of tuning this into a full length musical seemed to be the next step for the piece. Bernstein and Robbins wanted their friends to write the script and with George Abbott producing this became a given as well as the initial sale to MGM. (In the movie MGM only retained limited pieces of the original songs that Bernstein wrote).

Yet "On the Town" was based upon ballet and at that had a very detailed sexuality attached. "On The Town" was ripe with sexually aggressive woman and three sailors who were perhaps even too shy to comply but were certainly initially willing.

"On The Town" is truly an optimistically melancholy exuberant event. Three sailors on shore leave who are seeking to see New York City and at the same to see women as they see the sights is the plot. The women are at the same time looking for men.

Initially "On The town" was recognized for its multi-racial

and ethnic casting where there were black performers and Asian performers evident in the cast. Like "Oklahoma" it integrated fully characterization song dance and storytelling. As noted in a recent "Vanity Fair" article it integrated a"fresh contemporary hybrid—a genre mixing slapstick, book and nimble heartfelt lyrics.

If interested in those that auditioned and did not make the cut were Marlon Brando and a fresh out of the navy Kirk Douglas. Nancy Walker played the sex starved taxi driver, Comden and Greene themselves took two parts they had written for themselves. The song "Some Other Time" exemplified the heart ache that when in love sometimes time is precious.

~

Carousel

So how would Rodgers and Hammerstein do a follow up to Oklahoma? They searched for vehicles and came upon a sure fire winner.

There had been for some time the desire to take the Molnar play "Liliom" and convert it to a musicalized form. The first attempt was offered to Puccini, but Molnar was concerned that then that the play would always be remembered as Puccini's' "Liliom" and not Molnar's.

Initially the work was considered to be very depressing and not suitable for a musical, yet Rodgers and Hammerstein saw that an uplifting ending and more hopeful approach could develop this into a more suitable property.

The two worked to create several new inventions.

As had been their habit they fully integrated the dialogue and lyrics of the songs, yet in "Carousel" they took that even further with the development of a 12 minute sequence often referred to as the bench scene. In this scene the song "If I Loved You" is interwoven with dialogue and into musical phrase so keenly executed that if you are not listening closely you do no hear where the music ends and the dialogue continues. In recordings one hears "If I loved You" totally sung through, however in the real context of the script it is not sung through as one piece. This approach was a new invention.

Another new invention was the "Soliloquy" .Billy Bigelow the main character learns that he is to become a father. When the reality of this hits him he realizes that he must provide for a child. His revelation of this is discussed in an eight minute musical soliloquy, perhaps the first of its kind in a musical. It is dramatic, heartfelt, and the "thinking out loud" is revealing characterization.

The musical also explores, as a theme of Rodgers and Hammerstein classicism and bigotry. The rise of the bourgeoisie, as characterized by Carrie Pippperidge and Mr. Snow, demonstrates how the industrialization of New England created a society of "haves" and "have nots". The sadness of Billy and Julie's daughter, being scorned because of the social position and tragedy of Billy's life add a tragic yet redeemed opportunity in the creative story telling.

Agnes DeMille once again creates a dream ballet sequence to tell the story of this young girl and presents once again significant use of ballet in a musical for storytelling.

The style of characterization also began to become formulaic here. The use of a matriarchal figure who sings an anthem of hope (You'll Never walk alone") and the secondary somewhat comic love story as had been done in "Oklahoma!" became a further developed trademark foundation of the way their stories developed.

Stephen Sondheim tells the story that when he was a teenager Oscar Hammerstein allowed him to accompany him and his wife to the opening. Mrs. Hammerstein evidently always wore the same fur coat to an opening as a good luck charm. Sondheim tells how he sobbed so hard that he put his face into the sleeve of her coat and ruined the color from his tears.

When viewed today "Carousel" can be appreciated as far darker and serious, almost an operatic piece; more so than it was in its original conception.

~

Annie Get Your Gun

While Ethel Merman was recovering from a Cesarean birth Dorothy Fields and Jerome Kern had embarked on an idea to create a musical about Annie Oakley. They approached her and she thought it a terrific idea. Rodgers and Hammerstein turned the project down but thought that they would produce it as it seemed to be a potential hit but not their style of creative focus.

Jerome Kern suddenly had a stroke and died. The project was committed and they needed another composer. They sought out Irving Berlin. Berlin was not sure he could write for the new style of book musical and came back with several great songs that were included in the musical.

This became one of the most important roles Ethel Merman ever took on. This became the quintessential modern era role for her and she only missed two weeks for a vacation and per her usual only very rarely missed a performance.

"Annie" may not have set the musical onto new territory but it was a vastly entertaining event that created multiple pop chart standards. Irving Berlin once again created a Broadway musical that was current and modern.

For this reason plus adding Ethel Merman into the mix, "Annie Get Your Gun" became a classic of the era and certainly a musical we all can cherish.

The material written at the time was not considered politically correct in the 1999 revival starring Bernadette Peters and followed by Reba Macintyre. This could be disputed, but the heirs agreed that the way Indians were being portrayed in the script was less than desirable and changes were made to eliminate some very cartoonish character approaches.

~

Kiss Me Kate

Cole Porter had not had a hit of magnitude in recent years and the idea first developed by Rodgers and Hart to turn Shakespeare into a musical appealed to him. He liked the idea of turning "The Taming of the Shrew" into a musical.

Since "Oklahoma!" had opened and the integrated musical had evolved Cole Porter wanted to create a sophisticated option. He quipped that he could do by himself what it took two to do (a slam to Rodgers and Hammerstein).

The result was a show within a show concept of a bickering off stage couple and their attempt to mount a musical production of the "Taming of the Shrew."

The musical was brilliantly crafted; the show within the show had a musical numbers matching in the modern day backstage scenes.

Cole Porter who was a master in list songs created a masterful front of the curtain song "Brush Up Your Shakespeare" that had two gangsters punning their way through a list of Shakespearean plays to multiple nightly encores. In addition the sophisticated lyrics were full of the usual Cole Porter double entendre. The show ran over 1000 performances and was made into a 1953 movie that somewhat changed the script but kept much of the score.

The 1999 revival was the first major revival of "Kiss Me Kate" in 40+ years and based upon the original was slightly updated to make the plot more current. The production was so valued that it was filmed for PBS with the London cast that was playing at the time.

In March of 2015, the original cast recording was chosen by the Library of Congress to be included in its outstanding recording series.

~

South Pacific

This groundbreaking musical was based upon James A Michener's "Tales of the South Pacific", a collection of 19 stories that served as a catalyst for what would become "South Pacific". The book was merely a jumping off point and one story in particular was the basis of what would ultimately become the source material of the musical.

That particular story was that of Lt. Cable and the character Bloody Mary who wanted to wed her daughter to the marine. Cable ultimately realizes that his prejudice would not allow him to take this native girl back to America. He dies in a mission, but this one story was the birth of what was to come.

Another story that was put to good use was the story of a young woman from Arkansas who falls in love with a French planter. Another was the story about a Boars Tooth. The character of Luther Billis was woven through and the character became a source of comic relief.

Yet, in the real stories Emile had many children by various women and this was dropped for the musical for simplicity and more acceptable story telling

Also dropped for the overall plan was the use they had

now achieved of using ballet to tell the story. They did not want to have a version of "Madame Butterfly" so over time the emphasis of the story shifted to become what is now. A vision of the boredom of war, waiting for the enemy, then the issues that faced several characters in their reactions to racial issues became the core of the musical.

The idea of casting Pinza was a complicated bit of business getting him out of a previous contract and interesting him in this project. He wanted a more interesting career and was looking for challenges. However once signed on he was specific about not singing more than 15 minutes in a performance! The fact that they had Pinza; they then made this the leading male role, not Lt. Cable.

They also were very much a fan of Mary Martin who was touring in "Annie Get Your Gun". It was clear that she was the perfect candidate to be Nellie Forbush. She was worried that Pinza would overpower her singing voice and she asked that they not truly sing together which was ultimately the case.

Once this part was cast the script took shape showcasing the talents of the two leads. She did in fact come up with the idea to wash her hair on stage nightly and she also too singing "Wonderful Guy" sang the last measures in one breath a trait she carried to the stage with her performance.

The camaraderie on the production was strong yet Joshua Logan was a very demanding director and set very high expectations. His idea that there would be no real blackouts and the one scene would lead into another was quite groundbreaking at the time. It created a fluid story in motion.

Of course it is famous theatre rhetoric that the Song "You've Got to Be Carefully Taught "was a concern for the producers. There was a battle for the song were to be cut, (one excuse being the length of the show at the time, and the other being that the song would insult the audience). Rodgers and Hammerstein were so connected to the message that they refused to cut it and would have closed the show had it been the final verdict. Of course the song remained and the Pulitzer Prize for Drama was part of the accolades the play received because of that song.

"South Pacific "was a major game changer of the era and still packs its punch even today.

9 Best Musicals of the 1950's

- ☆ *My Fair Lady*
- ☆ *Gypsy*
- ☆ *West Side Story*
- ☆ *Guys and Dolls*
- ☆ *The Music Man*
- ☆ *The King and I*
- ☆ *Wonderful Town*
- ☆ *The Pajama game*
- ☆ *Damn Yankees*

My Fair Lady

Everyone has their personal favorites but Kitty Carlisle once shared that Fritz Loewe, as she called him, told her he was going to write the perfect musical out of "Pygmalion". The truth was that others had looked at the material and could not quite get a handle on how that would translate to a musical because of the theme of classism in Britain.

After Rogers and Hammerstein turned it down Lerner and Loewe picked it up and looked at the source, material. The 1937 movie of "Pygmalion" with Leslie Howard seemed to have the correct spirit for the script they needed to write and in fact created the musical themes that would ultimately become "My Fair Lady."

They wrote this on "spec", so to speak, as a major movie studio was looking at it also, and their "spec" version ultimately prevailed for Broadway production.

Moss Hart who had used the idea of revolving turntables in "Lady in the Dark" (1940) thought of that idea again and thought that was a great idea for "My Fair Lady".

The idea if course of Rex Harrison as Henry Higgins was certainly challenging as well. He really did not sing, but they created a musical chat sing style that certainly gained him wide acclaim and created a future style and approach for the character of Henry Higgins that has lived on for quite some time. (Recently Arena Stage in Washington DC cast an actor who actually sang the notes rather than the talk sing and it was totally disarming as it just was not the way you expected to hear Henry Higgins Sound).

There was also the idea of Eliza Doolittle. Julie Andrews who was a young ingénue, just recently had successful for her role in Sandy Wilson's British import and satire "The Boy Friend". She was cast. Moss Hart noted that she was often wooden truly not as developed an actress yet as he might have wished for but the glorious coloratura voice and precise diction she possessed were winning assets.

Of course the play opened to raves perhaps unheard for quite some time, and "My Fair Lady" with its delicious score became instantly popular.

The problem of getting everyone out of their ball attire was a challenge in Act II. There needed to be a time where everyone could simply get undressed and change. The challenge of course became what to do in front of the curtain while scenery and clothes were changed. A minor character that has an infatuation with Eliza gets a terrific break. Lerner and Loewe wrote a phenomenal front of the curtain song that instantly became a top 40 hit, "On The Street Where You Live". What a great gift they gave us.

"My Fair Lady" of course, over time became the musical that would run longer than "Oklahoma!" (the longest running musical at the time). It retained that record into the mid 1970's. Still it is so perfect and to many it is regarded as the most perfect musical ever written. Some authors even believe that Rex Harrison and Henry Higgins became one over time and some weren't sure where one began and the other as left off.

~

Gypsy

"Gypsy" is another great story. Whether it is Ben Brantley of the NY Times or Frank Rich Jr., there is little argument that "Gypsy" is among the greatest musicals ever written. Producer David Merrick became interested when Arthur Laurents realized it was the story of an overbearing mother trying to live through her children's life.

Irving Berlin and Cole Porter both turned it down (lucky for us). Jerome Robbins involved Stephen Sondheim to write the music and lyrics. However Ethel Merman, who needed a major hit at the time, did not want an unknown composer. Sondheim then refused and it was Oscar Hammerstein who convinced him to do the lyrics with Jule Styne as composer, who was the preference of Merman.

The character of Rose has been considered by some to be the King Lear of the American Musical. She can be seen to be a monster but as Stephen Sondheim has said she is not without redemption and in the end she confronts who she is and you see that she will work to have a relationship with her daughter who is the star Rose never became.

It's impossible to not love "Gypsy". The great lyrics, after all "once I was a schleppa now I'm miss Mazzeppa"—can't be better. Sondheim told the story of how they could not figure out an end to the goldstone song and rather than come up with a rhyme that was silly they all shout GOLDSTONE!

He related in a Kennedy Center interview, that they all went to see Cole Porter at Ethel Merman's insistence. Cole

Porter was not well, and upon hearing the lyric surprise he too was applauding the ingenuity of the lyrics.

It doesn't get much better than "Gypsy" frankly. You see emotion, parental choices and drive, not to mention that all of the major songs were written for Merman. Interestingly the part of Herbie doesn't sing much at all and there is only one true male song in the entire production. It is sung by a dancer who runs off with Baby June "All I Need is the Girl"—a fantastic number that packs a punch.

Recently "Playbill" asked on Facebook who was the best Mama Rose,—it's great that people debate that too!

~

West Side Story

If you have ever heard Hal Prince talk about "West Side Story" he says that everyone loves it now but they were the same people that walked out at intermission every night!

"Romeo and Juliet" provided a great background story for a tale that even today in gang driven communities' still resonates. There are still gang murders over turf and territory. Fortunately for us Arthur Laurents decided to abandon the initial premise of a Jewish boy and a Catholic girl over the Passover/Easter weekend. I think over time that would have become "a who cares at all". Gang rivalry still resonates in this day and age and the racism portion of the story still rings true.

"West Side" of course broke ground. In 1957 it was seriously violent. The first act ends with two murders. The second act ends with a third. This just did not happen in the 1950's in musicals. It is often said by Hal Prince that if you had not had "West Side Story" you would not have had "Fiddler" or "Cabaret".

In fact the two leading characters of "West Side" are more

of a larger part of an ensemble and frankly their music is wonderful, it is the ensemble approach with integrated dance that makes "West Side Story" soars.

Hearing Stephen Sondheim speak of this on several occasions he was not thrilled with the fact that all he could think of was to say Maria repeatedly as a song lyric, and he used to have to contain himself as he was never happy with "One Hand One Heart", Bernstein would be sobbing he once said and all he could do was run from the theater gagging over it.

"West Side Story" is too many a modern cornerstone of the contemporary musical we have today. Seeing it today it works and it is vivid, not stereotypical even if some of the characters don't give you a lot of meat to play with. The music still soars and is truly recognizable in an instant.

~

Guys and Dolls

There never really was the Times Square that Frank Loesser imagined with Abe Burrows but it was certainly a pretty exhilarating one. It is based upon two Damon Runyon Stories and Burrows heavily formed characters and moments from other stories as well.

Sadly, a victim of the times "Guys and Dolls" was selected to win the Pulitzer Prize for drama that year but because of Abe Burrows being called before the HUAC the award was withdrawn and no award was given for drama that year. What the implication of that is proves that something good can survive and be applauded. The top 40 hits shortly after opening included 5 songs from "Guys and Dolls". The characters changed the way people on stage talked.

Think about the lyrics, “Sue me, Sue Me, what can you do me, I love you.....”

Or”the average unmarried female, basically insecure”

“What’s playing at the Roxy, I’ll tell you what’s playing at the Roxy”: etc.

This is what makes “Guys and Dolls” what it is.

Ironically it was compared to “Pal Joey” which has long since languished and is rarely done today. Abe Burrows and Frank Loesser created a lovable heap of characters that still resonate with warmth and humor.

~

The Music Man

The minute I hear the full brass beat in the opening strains of “The Music Man” and then the spoken to rhythm song of the sales people on the train you are aware that this is a different take on Americana in a musical. The lead character is a scoundrel, although a loving one and the town librarian Marian Perue sees right through him.

Meredith Wilson took an agonizingly long time to write this chronicle of growing up in small town Iowa but set upon the task with aplomb and vigor.

Using a barber shop quartet and strong “spoofish” characterization he created a charming, smile a minute vehicle.

It is hard to believe that some producers did not want Robert Preston at all and that he had to beg for the part putting it into his contract that he could be fired on 48 hours’ notice. Some producer somewhere had a vision of Cary Grant as Harold Hill and frankly who could imagine that.

The King and I

Take a Diva of huge proportions and a determination to do something and you end up with "The King and I".

Gertrude Lawrence a well-regarded diva with a limited vocal range had become determined that the book Anna and the King of Siam was a sure fire vehicle for her. She approached Rodgers and Hammerstein who were truly reluctant.

Where was the love story? Rogers and Hammerstein saw nothing in the novel that they liked as a basis for a musical. They also preferred to make stars rather than to hire them and Gertrude Lawrence was a formidable well recognized grand diva. Lawrence was not also a great singer and yet they admired her acting skills, as Hammerstein called "her magic light" and ultimately agreed to write the show.

Forget any historical accuracy, but Rodgers and Hammerstein still focused on racial issues as part of the story, in addition to creating a love story between two secondary characters. After all the King and Mrs. Anna were not going to have an affair. The secondary couple gave the team the ability to write simply beautiful love songs.

In reality the perception was the king was a supporting role to Mrs. Anna and they wanted Rex Harrison who had originated the role in the movie. He was unavailable so a search continued. They then thought Alfred Drake and he made demands the team thought were excessive. How many divas does one creative team need? The discovery of Yul Brynner as the King was referred to them by Mary Martin. Yul Brynner made the play fly to those that ultimately reviewed it.

Gertrude Lawrence was frequently ill and had terrible performance issues. She fainted after a performance and found that upon entering a hospital she had long undiagnosed liver cancer. Yul Brynner now was the true star of the "King and I". At the insistence of Lawrence his name went to the top. When she died the lights of Broadway were dimmed, and she was buried in the dress she wore in the "Shall We Dance" number.

~

Wonderful Town

Many people don't put this on lists of bests.

I can't quite agree. After all look who the creative team was!

Comden and Greene and Leonard Bernstein! The book by Jerome Chodorov and Joseph Fields. It also was the re-invention of Rosalind Russell.

It is a combination of previous versions of "My Sister Eileen" that was restructured for the musical. It is rarely done today and because a movie was never made based upon the MGM annihilation of "On The Town" musically, Bernstein refused. Yet, with Rosalind Russel in tow, and knowing that she had a limited vocal range the music that was written suited her and they had a success.

The reviews of her performances were ecstatic and her husband Freddie Brisson made sure that she was well handled. An odd note is that he was referred to as the Lizard of Roz (by Ethel Merman), but the focus on her career paid off well into the next 20 years of her life. This totally changed her versatility and even gave here the lead in the "Gypsy" movie (hence Ethel's' nickname). When you look at "Wonderful Town" the music is not as familiar as other compositions Bernstein wrote, and the fact that Carol Channing closed the run playing that part for 6 months is a little known fact of the history, yet the musical with the Comden and Green lyrics is witty and clever.

Having never been made in to a film probably keeps it a bit under the radar but still this deserves to be mentioned as a great piece of the era.

~

The Pajama Game

Novels with unusual subject matter were becoming fodder for musicals. "Pajama Game" was based upon the labor dispute in a Midwestern pajama factory over a 71/2 cent raise and the implications of the shop steward and the foreman having a developing romantic relationship.

Well one could say what's the big deal, but in the mid 50's this was new territory and once again the hit parade of songs that emerged from the wonderful score emerged. "Hernandos' Hideaway", "Steam Heat", and the wonderfully conceived "Hey There" were recorded often. The idea of singing a duet into a Dictaphone was new and very cutting edge for a Broadway musical at the time. Rosemary Clooney made a very famous recording released shortly after the opening of the musical getting it on the pop charts quickly.

Adler and Ross wrote a great score and the show just had a naughty blue collar sophistication. Add to this the Bob Fosse choreography and" Pajama Game" launched a new era. "Steam Heat" with derby hats, and cocked waists became the newly recognizable Fosse style.

There is the other discovery! A young Shirley MacLaine had been Carol Haney's understudy and while Carol Haney was out recovering from a broken ankle Hal Wallis (the movie producer) discovered Shirley and the rest is history there as well.

"Pajama Game" too could be argued about, was it really that good? The movie with Doris Day certainly captures it and frankly seemed cutting edge at the time. It is still enjoyable and worth watching. It is a true pleasure of the era.

~

Damn Yankees

Faust as a musical? Really?

The novel, The Year the Yankees Lost the Pennant certainly created the opportunity to become a musical and I grew up singing "You've Gotta Have Heart".

Growing up in DC and knowing that the Washington Senators never won a ball game was exciting for an emerging Broadway musical geek. I even found out that the action sometimes took place in Chevy Chase nearby where I lived. Now that was just too cool. Evidently the novel was somewhat dismissed, but having Ray Walston as the devil and Gwen Verdon as his siren was terrific.

A secret many are not aware of there is a secondary actress in a minor character part who sings a reprise of "Heart". It is none other than Jean Stapleton who went on to play Edith Bunker in "All in the Family" years later.

Some could argue this one as well, but a baseball musical had never successfully been done and this once again proved that during this era something jazzy and exciting could become something special.

"Damn Yankees" solidified Gwen Verdon as a major star and performer. An often forgotten moment is that in the movie version which is truly faithful to the original has the song "Who's Got the Pain". In the movie version the song is danced by Gwen Verdon with non-other than Bob Fosse himself. As they leave the "stage" Tab Hunter as Joe Hardy in the wings says "great job Fosse". I never caught it until recently, but it's there to see even on YouTube.

10 Best Musicals of the 1960's

- ☆ *Fiddler On The Roof*
- ☆ *Cabaret*
- ☆ *Oliver*
- ☆ *Funny Girl*
- ☆ *Hello Dolly*
- ☆ *1776*
- ☆ *Hair*
- ☆ *Sound OF Music*
- ☆ *A Funny Thing Happened on the way to the Forum*
- ☆ *She Loves Me*

Fiddler on the Roof

It has been mentioned earlier that if "West Side Story" had not happened with its tragic ends to both of its acts you might not have had "Fiddler on the Roof".

Bock and Harnick had been discussing the idea of taking the Tevye stories and converting them into a musical. That project got terribly side tracked over the early 1960's and they ended up doing "She Loves Me" first, but the idea of doing these stories to music seemed ideal.

At first the script had a different focus as it even centered more on the five daughters more than it did around Tevye. The focus on how generational viewpoints could change and challenge those of the older generation, although central to the story, was not recognized as the musical was being written."Fiddler" in its gestation could not have been imagined to have become what it became. The idea of life in a Russian village at the turn of the 20th century was not imagined to be necessarily universal in appeal, the shtetl life certainly would resonate with the Jewish audience, but could it have a wider range of interest? It was certainly doubtful.

Yet the universal story of how the traditions of an older generation can be challenged by the young took a story and set it in motion.

There were many arguments about how the story should be told.

Jerome Robbins saw the vision, and there were the complicated discussions of how the opening number should be positioned. It was first about the daughters, but slowly as the focus became clear, the emphasis on challenges to the trusted traditions of the elders became obvious to Bock and Harnick. The classic opening number "Tradition" added the deeply needed anchor to the story. In eight minutes you knew the village, the characters, the lifestyle and above all, the ability to recognize what this story was about. The opening number framed the story.

Let's be honest this is not a light happy story. The bigotry of Tsarist Russia that evicted communities of Jewish people from their homes is not a happy one, yet with the larger than life character that Tevye became as an anchor to demonstrate how people cope with change the story was set into motion.

"Fiddler" changed story telling form. From its' Chagall inspired sets to its honest portrayal of a people that were sent out for truly no reason the impact of forced change on a community still is fresh and relevant now 50 years later, as it was when it was written.

The music was not that of the style that was being written in other successful musicals of the time, but its ability to pull upon the style of eastern European music as thematic approach set it apart. How many weddings still have tears flow from the strains of "Sunrise Sunset"? The song, so simply sung, so totally honest, and relevant tells, many generational truths. It is fair to say that the audience starts to cry about a third of the way through Act I and continues until the end of the musical. It's just great theatre.

~

Cabaret

Hal Prince liked ambitious undertakings!

"Cabaret" is a story that uses two versions of an earlier work to reinvent story telling. The John Van Dreuten play " I Am a Camera" was a basis but the Berlin Stories which served as the catalyst for that play were a more richly followed source for "Cabaret".

Think about it. Who would imagine a musical play centered on the rise of Nazism in 1931 Berlin to be material for a musical? Mel Brooks even spoofed it in "The Producers". Yet the team with Hal Prince at the helm and with Kander and Ebb and Joe Masterhoff creating the book something different was truly afoot.

The use of an on stage all female band, the use of a symbolic character as the MC, who truly represented evil, a bisexual character (although toned down for the 1966 version) the well-presented anti-Semitism of the time all were unique and in many ways presented creatively and originally. Who would imagine this would have the roots to become one of the greatest musicals of all time.

Yet even with provocative, clever storytelling, the characters who resigned themselves to a horrible future, all too clearly resonated.

Even the theme song "Cabaret", sung by Sally Bowles, who avoided looking at the realities around her, is not heard as the joyous number it has become when lifted out of context. Rather it is a sad explanation of why she must just continue to plod along in her usual method. "Cabaret" continued the style of musical story telling that "West Side" and "Fiddler" developed. Interesting views on tragic circumstances told to music.

~

Oliver

You can't ignore this that this was revolutionary in its time.

British musicals had never crossed the Atlantic successfully, and here was a Dickens novel with all of its Victorian pages coming to life as a musical.

Let's be clear the story was a bit simplified for the stage and the portrayal of Fagin and made more a comic villain than the anti-Semitic portrayal that Dickens chose, but without "Oliver" we may never have had the musicals of the 1980's and forward that used deep novels as their basis.

"Oliver" also had terrific music, a unique story telling approach and above all a new vision of how to use a stage to tell a story. The set that was made of wooden boxes that twisted and turned to create London of the time was revolutionary and set ideas into motion.

It may not be one of the best and most memorable of the era, but it set forth an opportunity for future storytelling to music that would not have happened without it. In its own way it was revolutionary and groundbreaking both for its music and design.

The score was on the radio; "As Long as He Needs Me" becoming a big hit, and also performed the night The Beatles made their American debut on Ed Sullivan.

Funny Girl

When you think about all of the musicals that were destined not to be, this surely is one of them.

Suddenly musicals about famous people were in vogue, certainly after “Gypsy”, “The Sound of Music”, “Fiorello”, and “The Unsinkable Molly Brown”. This was a genre that seemed to always work. “Funny Girl” was not the easiest task to create as by this time in the mid-sixties Fanny Brice was potentially a forgotten legend and the rags to riches with heartbreak story had to be framed in a believable way.

The authors fought about approach and they couldn’t find an actress that they all agreed upon to portray Fanny Brice.

It was plagued with disasters. The whole idea initially started as a movie idea before Broadway was imagined as Ray Stark thought his mother in laws’ story made great movie music material. The shift to the Broadway realm had Garson Kanin leading the parade, writing the script, which was later finished by Isobel Lennart. It was challenging to say the least. The focus was muddy and argued over at length.

Originally Stephen Sondheim was to do the lyrics with Jule Styne until someone thought Mary Martin might make a great Fanny Brice. Well that sent Stephen Sondheim running. Among those they considered and could not secure included, Anne Bancroft, Edye Gorme, Carol Burnett, and a few others. Streisand surfaces and of course the rest is history.

Yet, Streisand too many resembled a young Fanny Brice, had qualities missing that Fanny possessed. Many recalled that Fanny had a sexy sly coy demeanor. Even though she was not a beauty in her persona there was that certain “je ne sais qua”! This had to be created somehow with Streisand who obviously rose to the occasion.

In the Book **Roadshow** by Matthew Kennedy there is much written about the feud that was started over the Tony award honors between Streisand and Carol Channing? One can debate which of the two musicals “Hello Dolly” or “Funny Girl” was better, but the nods went to Dolly and it’s hard to fathom that Streisand did not achieve the Best Actress Honor. The feud was only exasperated by the “Hello Dolly” movie casting.

Listening to the original cast recording one hears several terrific “errors”. Had Barbra had control over the recording some would never been allowed to be heard. In the song “Coronet Man” she elides the lyric ‘WAWA MUTE into WAWAMUE.” The other is at the end of “Don’t Rain on My Parade” she cracks. The great thing about this is, you get to hear that she isn’t always perfect and before she sought out and took control there were flaws. These are the flaws that many performers live with and make the recording all that much more interesting. Today these flaws never occur.

One wonderful surprise for the unaware is that a supporting role in Funny Girl on stage (Mrs Strakosh) was handled with her unique style by Jean Stapleton. It can be forgotten that Jean Stapleton was an accomplished Broadway character actress and had done several musicals including “Damn Yankees” and “Bells Are Ringing”. She can be heard in her pre Edith Bunker days loud and clear in several places in this recording. You see you never know where people have been hiding!

One final note! It’s never been revived on Broadway. Maybe it is the stardom that it created and perhaps that it is so closely connected to Barbra Streisand that no one has truly ever tackled it. What actress would want the comparison?

Hello Dolly

This has to be on the list because for the rest of the decade "Hello Dolly" infiltrated our culture. Yes it too had a checkered history.

If you were hiding under a rock you may have missed that Jerry Herman, Gower Champion with Producer David Merrick had set out to make a musical of Thornton Wilders " The Matchmaker" which itself was a remake of a play "The Merchant of Yonkers."

Shirley Booth had of course done the play and the movie with Anthony Perkins and Robert Morse to great success.

This Thornton Wilder play seemed like a natural for a musical. At first it was being written for Ethel Merman. She had just finished her run in Gypsy including a nationwide tour and she knew that commitment to a new musical would be years and years. She needed a break. She told Jerry Herman that she would close it for them. When she said that it probably didn't not occur to her that it would be several years away before that actually happened? She did close the show and they added back two songs that were written for her and cut from the Channing version.

After Merman said no, everyone wanted Mary Martin and she turned it down. Ultimately after some searching they selected Carol Channing who truthfully since 1949 had not introduced a character in a musical. She did a lot of great comedy work, especially with George Burns upon Gracie Allen's retirement, but carrying a new musical was new to her. She also had her specific style. David Burns a character actor himself was chosen as Horace. The book of 'Dolly" isn't exactly double decker drama. It is cute, lively and almost an extended minstrel show. It's just plain adorable, and fun, yet not terribly logical but great entertainment.

Once the show opened in Detroit it became clear that it just was not working and that the flimsy somewhat odd plot had not a focus on Dolly (BTW it had the title "Dolly Levi a Very Exasperating Woman") and the title role focus was shining on Horace Vandergelder not the character of Dolly Levi. As the run in Detroit came to a close David Merrick considered pulling the plug. Everyone knew it was just not working. Toward the very end of the run the vision that the Dolly character had to be the focus became clear and the song "Before the Parade Passes by" was written as a first act closing for Dolly. The story then took on a different shape and suddenly the focus changed.

Dolly still had ridiculous plot conventions enhanced by wonderful Gower Champion choreography that was almost airborne in the Second Act "Hello Dolly" Number. This after all created the famous "Waiter's Gallup". Yet the crowning pre-opening achievement pushed Dolly into the stratosphere. Louis Armstrong recorded the title song and boom! The song caught on quickly.

Arriving in DC shortly after Detroit, in a terrible time, after the Kennedy assassination, the glitter of it all suddenly appealed. Even Lyndon Johnson went to see it. "Hello Dolly", became a part of the 60's culture. Even at the Democratic Convention of 1964, "Hello Lyndon" was sung to the tune of "Hello Dolly". "Hello Dolly" of course out ran the run of "My Fair Lady" and achieved truly icon status for both itself and the star. Carol Channing played it over 4000 times over years, and even Mary Martin took it to London.

It was played by every faded movie queen you could remember from Betty Grable, Dorothy Lamour, to Phyllis Diller. Of course in 1967 the cast was changed to an all-black cast starring Pearl Bailey and Cab Calloway. That put it back in to a new version and jump started it all over again. In retrospect why it had to be an all-black cast is still ridiculous, but at the time it was considered a genius of an idea.

~

1776

In 1968, the country was war torn. Demonstrations about the war were everywhere and then in the end of 1960's who would have imagined that a musical based upon the writing of the Declaration of Independence would be recognized as a success. It was hard to also believe it was suspenseful and rousing.

Written by Peter Stone with words and music by Sherman Edwards this musical written with John Adams as its lead character and with an almost all male cast, somehow had the appeal that it had. Many historical issues are not correct and the characters involved are not historically accurate but the semi historical satirical jovial atmosphere making fun at times of the founding fathers was refreshing and at the same time entertaining

It is more of a comment on the time, and yet even with its historical liberties still remains a breakthrough moment in the presentation of a historical musical with real context and purpose. As has been often said the minute you hear "Sit Down John" in the opening lyrics you know are in for a different sort of historical evening.

Betty Buckley made her big part premiere as Abigail Adams, and John Cullum who took over as Rutledge gave such an iconic performance that he was cast in the very faithful film version. The times could not have indicated that this could have even been a success and that it ran three + years truly make it an iconic musical of the times.

A Funny Thing Happened on the Way to the Forum

This is important and iconic for so many reasons. One favorite reason is that it is the first of the Sondheim musicals where he did it all. It may not have the developed wonderful music and lyrics he created for his later outstanding musicals but certainly anything Sondheim is close to perfect.

The plays of Plautus were the basis for this ribald, silly, over the top musical that featured Zero Mostel with choreography by Jerome Robbins. The two never spoke based upon history they both had with the McCarthy era and were only engaged via third parties. Yet to get a show mounted both agreed to work together even if it was not in a cordial environment.

The musical tried out in Washington, DC to less than enthusiastic reviews. As has been shared time and time again by Sondheim and others the opening number "Love is in the Air" was telling the wrong story to the audience. The plot of "Forum" is really about the antics of the slave Psuedelous and his attempts to buy his freedom.

As Sondheim has said on numerous occasions "if you have a good opening number you can fool an audience for at least 45 minutes". That being known George Abbott and Jerome Robbins both knew that a new opening number was needed. The audience needed to know from the start that this was to be a funny evening of robust low humor. The result of course was the brilliant opening "Comedy Tonight" choreographed with genius skill by Jerome Robbins became. It set the new tone and the audience suddenly got the idea at the start.

The entire musical came together from that. "Forum" is one of those musicals that take comic nuance and great broad stroke ability. Everyone who has ever taken the role of

Psuedelous has had great acclaim form Zero, to Phil Silvers, Jason Alexander and Nathan Lane. Maybe this was not the greatest musical of the era, but it launched Sondheim from being just a lyricist to a true Broadway composer. It has earned a place on this list.

~

Hair

The "love-in" that was "Hair" changed everything about Broadway musicals and they have recovered slowly. "Hair" was irreverent, focused on the young "Hippie" audience of the era and based upon its rock score a very different sounding musical. Cast members came out of the audience, used a hand mike to sing their music, used what was considered at the time atrocious language and of course how can we forget to comment on the landmark nude scene?

The challenge from "Hair" was that now many creative teams were pondering how to create Rock Musicals and none ever achieved the status that "Hair" reached. It also has the distinction of being the last Broadway musical for 14 years to have songs reach the top 40 pop charts. (Not until Cats! with the song "Memory" did that fact change with very few if any that can be thought of since.)

In truth, although it was recently revived to capture the memory of aging baby boomers, it is a museum piece of the time. It still had energy and its resonance of a time but it also seemed almost quaint. I laughed recently when a friend Cliff Lipson shared with me that when he was in the "Hair" at the time Broadway scale was what he got paid plus and additional $1.85 for the nude scene which was optional. Doing it 8 times a week every week added almost $80.00 to his paycheck and paid the rent!

12 Best Musicals of the 1970's

- ☆ *Company*
- ☆ *Follies*
- ☆ *A Little Night Music*
- ☆ *The Candide Revival*
- ☆ *A Chorus Line*
- ☆ *Chicago*
- ☆ *Ain't Misbehavin*
- ☆ *No No Nanette revival*
- ☆ *Gypsy Revival*
- ☆ *Evita*
- ☆ *Grease*
- ☆ *Sweeney Todd*

Company

In 1970 in the midst of the sexual revolution a musical about marriage was an interesting choice of material. Do not forget this was the same year the movie "Bob, Carol, Ted and Alice" took place not to mention the growing up of the cinema into adult story telling as the sixties ended.

Stephen Sondheim landed upon George Furth's one act plays or skits about marriage in New York. A 35 year old bachelor, examining the foibles of the relationships of his friends, and reacting to them is the crux of the script. There is not a plot exactly at all which was the continuation of the concept musical form that started with "Hair". Of course in the present day a 35 year old unmarried guy is not so unusual, but back in the dawn of the 1970's it did seem odd and culturally detached. Much has been written about how Bobby (the lead character) is just an observer to the goings on. Yet he in fact becomes a Greek chorus of one and comments obliquely on the relationships of his friends.

It does not feel dated perhaps because of the genius of the music, the truth in which relationships are portrayed and the resonance that this was a great beginning for the Sondheim era.

Listening to that recording still does give many great hours of listening. The recording was part of a planned documentary series that CBS had planned. The idea was to film the recording sessions of other Broadway musicals. Filming these personalities involved showed how pressure to preserve for posterity the music of the musical became challenging. The egos, the defeats of agony to not be perfect enough, the passion of the composer are all in the spotlight. To hear Elaine Stritch in agony that she cannot get her monumental number correctly sung is courageous and at the same time almost pitiful to see. Of course no other such documentary was ever filmed but this is one to cherish. It is also interesting to see how "dressed up" the Broadway work atmosphere looked in 1970! The attire alone that people wore to record in a studio is a far cry from today's attire.

"Company" has so many musical delights that to list them too would be another list for this book. To know it is to love it. This concept musical that has flourished ever since, has had its' hand in killing the traditional book musical. A Broadway musical may have many styles now.

~

Follies

In the summer of 1972, we made a choice to see the Tony production winner for best musical for 1972 and it was not "Follies". To this day I still cannot believe that we saw "Two Gentleman of Verona" (the actual winner) instead. Yes Sondheim won for best music and lyrics, but it took me about 25 more years to see a real production of "Follies" as it was deemed bookless, shallow and manipulative with music that was far better than the lame book, to paraphrase many attitudes of the critics then.

The idea for "Follies" is based upon a picture of Gloria Swanson standing in the ruble of the Roxy Theater in New York. The idea further created a reunion of old "Follies" girls, and frames the basis for the story as they come together to lie, share their histories, and recall their glory days. The musical numbers all written as pastiche of musical numbers from another era reveal their frailties, serving as a backdrop for a star crossed love story from years ago. It also points out the choices we make and the pain the choices sometimes cause.

The Clive Barnes review in the "New York Times" highlighted the great confusion about the piece. Stylish, innovative" and "a serious attempt to deal with the musical form." Yet he thought it was taking "nostalgia to the point where it engulfs it in its sticky maw."

Ted Chapin of the Hammerstein organization has written a great book about "Follies" as he was a 20 year old "gofer" on the production and it is amazing to see what it was and what changed.

Hal Prince and Michael Bennet shared directing credits for the $750,000 musical, the first time a choreographer shared directing credits. The costs, which were considered outrageous, eclipsed Broadway budgets at the time. This may have even caused a built in resentment of it.

"Follies" has always been cast with the faded stars of another era. That was part of the conceit. It's not a requirement but it certainly adds a bit of faded glitz to the proceedings.

When it was first recorded RCA victor made the terrible decision to cut numbers so that the entire album would fit on one record. This was horrific because it shortened some songs and eliminated "One Last Kiss" entirely. To the fans of Sondheim this was a flaming dagger into the heart.

It took 15 years or so to get that great recording, done in concert and filmed as a documentary for all to see what went on behind the scenes of recording "Follies in Concert". In the many years since the "Follies" original run has become recognized as one of the great Sondheim masterpieces, not just a cult musical.

~

A Little Night Music

If you are a Sondheim fan this may be everyone's favorite among favorites!

The wonderful farcical story of long lost love and bad behavior among adults is delightful, charming, witty, and clever and above all features the most famous Sondheim song ever written.

It is the story of the romantic escapades of a myriad of couples and their romantic intertwining. It is exquisitely written and Clive Barnes in the New York Times called the musical "heady, civilized, sophisticated and enchanting." He noted that "the real triumph belongs to Stephen Sondheim... the music is a celebration of 3/4 time, an orgy of plaintively memorable waltzes, all talking of past loves and lost worlds... There is a peasant touch here." He commented that the lyrics are "breathtaking".[1]

As noted, the music was very unusual in its presentation for the Broadway stage. There were multiple trios, quintets, quartets, and true vocal hi-jinx as created in what has been referred to as a waltz musical. All of the music is written in a variation of ¾ time, something that had never before been done.

As almost an afterthought it became clear that the part of Desiree needed another song in the second act. The part was imagined that Desiree would actually not do much singing but in the second act the role required (as did the ego of Glynis Johns) a song to set straight the folly of her desires. As any composer can tell you if you know who you are writing for it is easy! Her ability to carry long phrases was limited so Sondheim wrote a song of short phrases all ending in consonants that would emulate the style of her speaking voice. A simple song of great disappointment and disillusionment become "Send in The Clowns".

Many musicals are referred to as perfect. "My Fair Lady" is one. To many others this is on that list as well. The characters are each well drawn, the actions are specific, the resolutions all appropriate. This is a musical that is perfectly crafted, not a moment on stage is wasted.

It is a favorite!

~

The Candide Revival

"Candide" is of course the great musical masterpiece that Bernstein wrote based upon Voltaire. The music and the lyrics were brilliant but the whole evening was dragged down by a heavy handed book that had little humor and direction that was too heavy for what needed to be light weight and satirical.

At the 1956 opening the music was lauded with great praise, but the book seemed to get tiresome and although the direction form Tyronne Guthrie was applauded the whole suffered under its weight.

Come 1973, Hal Prince took the idea that 'Candide "needed to be presented in a crazy, free spirited way capturing the Rock music style of "Hair". The audience sat on bleachers in a totally re-envisioned theater, proscenium thrown away and the balcony's blended into a stadium like effect.

The production was the start of a tinkering that has continued for decades. Even though in its' premiere run it suffered and died, the revival in 1973 gave life to a work that has now been performed by Opera companies worldwide. Bernstein continued to work on the piece until his death which had made "Candide" even more of a jewel.

The PBS live concert with Patti Lupone and Kristin Chenowith is a remarkable example of how exciting productions can become from disasters.

~

A Chorus Line

Michael Bennet wanted to create a memoir to the Broadway Gypsies. The Origin of "A Chorus Line" to this day has its own controversies, but the bottom line is that Michael Bennet took the stories of his dancer friends and the details of how they clung to dance adding the Marvin Hamlisch music, Ed Kleban and Bob Avian doing lyrics with the book by James Kirkwood, Jr. and Nicholas Dante.

The controversy is of course how the dancers who shared their life stories all signed away their rights to these stories for a pittance, as they were not made totally aware of the scope of the project. The result was that legal battles ensued.

"Thirty hours of taped recorded truths" are what Michael Bennett told the "NY Times" became the basis of "A Chorus Line". It became a mechanism that would be observed by the audience at a theoretical audition. No real audition has the time for the psychotherapy that is evident on stage during the course of the musical yet it seemed truly real.

All of that aside "A Chorus Line" produced by the Public Theatre Off Broadway, then in 1975 moved to the Shubert Theatre on Broadway where is ran for 6137 performances. It became a huge phenomenon and a version of the ultimate "Gotta sing-Gotta dance" stories that have been written for decades. The NY times said of it this was a version of "42nd Street" for a new generation.

"A Chorus Line" was a direct descendant of "Cabaret", "Company" and "Follies". Michael Bennett created something that advanced and set the concept musical art form into mainstream musical style. It was a phenomenon at the start.

It was unlike any other musical that had come before it. There were frank and heartfelt monologues discussing sexuality, child abuse, remaking ones' self for fame, plus plenty of heartbreak. Some thought this to be a depressing evening in the theatre, as at the time it was raw, biting and frank like nothing before it. Yet to most it was an exhilarating vibrant event. The idea that we are all on the line, auditioning every day created a deeper connection for the audience yet at the same time there was the important ability to see people win and lose.

Over time the musical, still wonderful, is more like a museum piece. You go to see a great painting and it becomes frozen in time by the artist, framed and hung on the wall to enjoy. There is nothing about "A Chorus Line" that today seems shocking as it did in 1975. The montages, the dialogue the song lyrics that were then so bold and truly unique are today much more common place situations. Yet when viewed this is still great theatre even though it can only be what it is and was.

~

Chicago

Opening against noise from another hyped musical can limit the charms of another hidden masterpiece. The public was not ready for the cynicism and point of view that was offered of our judicial system in 1975. Clive Barnes stated in his review "Chicago is one of those shows where a great deal is done with very little". He led the parade of people who did not quite comprehend the satire and bite that was "Chicago".

Chicago was based upon the movie "Roxie Hart" about the media and the justice system in 1920's Chicago.

The musical "Chicago" is based on a play of the same name by reporter and playwright Maurine Dallas Watkins, who was assigned to cover the 1924 trials of accused murderers Beulah Annan and Belva Gaertner for the *Chicago Tribune*. In the early 1920s, Chicago's press and public became riveted by the subject of homicides committed by women. Several high-profile cases arose, which generally involved women killing their lovers or husbands. These cases were tried against a backdrop of changing views of women in the Jazz age, and a long string of acquittals in Cook County, juries of women murderesses (jurors at the time were all men, and convicted murderers generally faced death by hanging).

In the 1960s, Gwen Verdon read the play and asked her husband, Bob Fosse, about the possibility of creating a musical adaptation. Fosse approached playwright Watkins numerous times to buy the rights, but she repeatedly declined. In her later years, Watkins had become very religious and believed her play glamorized a scandalous way of living. However, upon her death in 1969, her estate sold the rights to producer Richard Fryer, Verdon, and Fosse. Kander and Ebb began work on the musical score, modeling each number on a traditional vaudeville number or a vaudeville performer. This format made explicit the show's comparison between "justice", "show-business", and contemporary society. Ebb and Fosse penned the book of the musical, and Fosse also directed and choreographed in his signature style that is closely identified with the production.

The musical received mixed reviews. The Brechtian style of the show, made audiences uncomfortable. According to James Leve, "Chicago, is cynical and subversive, exploiting American cultural mythologies in order to attack American celebrity culture".

The other big new opening of the season (A Chorus Line) eclipsed "Chicago" with raves and Fosse of course created his new one minute TV spot for the new musical and had Gwen and Chita on every TV show imaginable. If you look at YouTube you can see them on any number of programs doing numbers from the show to build an audience. After 900+ performances it closed and rotted away into obscurity. By the early 1990's the original cast recording had gone out of print and was nowhere to be found.

The O.J. Simpson trial had changed attitudes about the press and its' impact on the trials. The cynicism that surrounded the original production seemed remotely accurate was now a vivid example of reality.

The Encores! Program, in 1996 at the City Center in New York, producing long forgotten musicals in the way the originals were meant to be seen and heard looked at "Chicago". The approach to Ann Reinking to help stage a concert version of Chicago (with the help of Gwen Verdon) became a reality. It was so positively received that producers Barry and Fran Weissler moved it to Broadway. The critics went wild, and it is still today running almost twenty years later. Unlike the predecessor of the 1970's this time there was universal praise for the production.

This also helped re-ignite the movie musical and in 2002 "Chicago" won best picture Oscar and a genre was reinvigorated. Time has an interesting perspective, some things that were praised in their day fade away and others that were not so loved can become benchmarks of a new era.

Chicago is a masterpiece and has achieved the status it deserves.

~

Ain't Misbehavin

We talk about genres being invented! This was an invention.

It is important to note that this may not really be the first Jukebox musical as "George M!" based upon the life and music of George M Cohan in 1968 certainly could claim that title, yet "Ain't Misbehavin" really does prove to be the first success where no story and just music propel an evening of entertainment in the theater.

The idea of taking the music of "Fats Waller" and setting in a Cotton Club like setting with 5 singers who all had a look that recognized the early nineteen forties Harlem was ingenious. There was no plot, almost no dialogue and a series of great songs put over by the five superior singers on stage. It is hard to imagine the genre bending idea that set the stage for many so called juke box musicals to come. It was simple, affordable to produce and mesmerizing in style. All of is it a great combination.

The high energy performance made a star out of Nell Carter. What was initially politely received by the audience turned quickly to aperture at the music and dance were often presented as small "skits" adding great interest to the proceedings.

As Richard Eder said in the New York Times Review

"what whistles hoots, throws off sparks and moves at 180 miles per hour? Its "Aint Misbehavin"

~

No! No! Nanette revival

This was also the era where producers were seeking new and interesting ways to fill seats. Black musicals, rock musicals and revivals musical were certainly three strategies that caught on. Why on earth would we talk about a creaky old musical from the 1920's? "NO! NO! Nanette", had two great Vincent Youmans songs "Tea for Two" and "I Want to be Happy", and a long forgotten tapping star Ruby Keeler in a dazzling production.

For the nostalgic 1971 Broadway revival conceived and produced by Harry Rigby, Burt Shevelove freely adapted the book from the 1925 original. While the 1925 book was considered quite racy at the time of the original production, Shevelove wrote from a nostalgic perspective, depicting the 1920s as a time of innocent fun. He made extensive changes and cuts to the book, but most of the original score was left intact, with only a few cuts and interpolations.

Ruby Keeler, the musical ingénue of the 1930 movie musicals returned from retirement for the production. She was lauded for energetic tap routines incorporated into "I Want to Be Happy" and "Take A Little One-Step".

The real excitement here was that "No! No! Nanette" created a genre that has become a Broadway staple ever since, the revival. This was not the first but it certainly was the first that brought forward something from another era and then became a major hit as a revival.

Gypsy with Angela Lansbury

London had never had a real production of "GYPSY" until 1973. Many were convinced that the Merman portrayal was the benchmark and that any actress approaching the role of Mama Rose was destined to be compared to it in every way possible.

Angela was not the first choice. It was scheduled to open with Elaine Stritch but she was not getting tickets sold and Angela was then put into replace her and tickets sold furiously. The vision of how Merman (and Rosalind Russell) played the role was quickly diminished. It became clear that Merman could not own a character forever and that this revival set a new tone—"Gypsy" just needs a powerhouse performance. The book and the score are so strong that with the right character in place by a skilled musical actress "Gypsy" can be re-invented again and again.

For no other reason besides that it was a magnificent revival, this production insured that Gypsy can be seen again and again in a fresh and new light.

~

Evita

British musicals had historically had a rough crossing when they came to the colonies! Many had not fared well and the young team of Tim Rice and Andrew Lloyd Weber had been working to change that.

"Evita", had originally been based upon a concept concert album and the idea of turning it into a full-fledged musical blossomed. The team had already had two imports achieve some attention, with "Jesus Christ Super" and "Joseph and the Amazing Technicolor Dreamcoat". Their style was the pop opera rather than the traditional book musical. The fully sung musical was now becoming an artistic option and this was their focus. The historical accuracy was debatable as the main resource for the script was based on an account from a book "Woman with a Whip" and the leanings were biased as written. However, good theatre does not rely on accuracy.

Eva Peron could be considered an interesting un-sympathetic choice for a musical heroine, hardly likable and even less charming. The story telling approach and the presentation drove the piece.

Hal Prince conceived a production that was non-stop in motion from the death sequence at the start and cast Elaine Page as Evita for the London cast. He wanted her for the New York cast but actors' equity denied the request. When Patti Lupone developed vocal challenges he tried to get her again. Patti Lupone herself claims this to have been the worst time of her life due to the demands of the role, but come on you become a major name because of this and you complain?

I do recall seeing the original several times as my college friend; Peter Marinos was cast in the chorus. Peter went on to play Evita's first boyfriend the singer Magaldi and played it at the National Theatre in DC while on tour. I recall him telling me that when he heard the opening sequence and the note that he had to keep singing for ten minutes he thought he might think this insanity, but seeing a friend in a production that was so incredible at the time was really wonderful.

It is interesting to recall thinking "Why do I like this so much when I hate the character?" It was the secret of the musical. The character was hideous but had quite a story...

Evita is a first of a different sort of musical. It takes the bio-musical that "Gypsy" and "Fiorello" created years earlier and creates a modern pop style opera musical. Although it didn't run for eons it has toured and has had much pop cultural success.

It belongs on the list as a game changer for sure.

~

Grease

When something becomes a Culutrual phenomenon you do have to give it respect. "Grease " in its' original format was a raunchy, vulgar sendup of a Chicago area high school reset into a blue collar area about the kids of the time called Greasers. It was not a "PG rated" musical at all yet because of the great success of the movie has been tamed down over time as it was far more accessible and one success fueled the other.

The plot follows ten working-class teenagers as they navigate the complexities of peer pressure, politics, personal core values, and love. There was teen pregnancy, the idea of dropping out of high school, becoming a" bad girl" to become better liked, all issues that are usual coming of age material, yet told in a semi-satirical style of the time with music that aped the sound of the era.

It is simple a successful revivable staple of the Broadway musical archive.

As it has been sanitized over the years to make it more family friendly that was not the basis of where it began. As a result this too became the most successful movie musical of an era and a generation grew up believing this was the vision of the 1950's they would recall.

This is a musical that took the vision of what "Bye Bye Birdie" was, played on the rising baby-boomer nostalgia for the period and ran with it. There are so many now revised forms of the script that 'Grease" has become a family theatre outing. It even used a reality show to cast a recent revival.

The 1950's were never really like this either, but "Grease" gives us a sense that it must have been.

~

Sweeney Todd

I have my favorites. It is controversial, challenging, articulate, creepy and best of all considered by most Stephen Sondheim's masterpiece. It is an acquired taste to some. Yet, under the direction of Hal Prince it demonstrated the evils of the industrial age in London with it blaring factory whistle, its metal factory like setting and of course the anger and miscarriages of justice that were prevalent at the time.

When appearing in it once myself, I was struck by something. Each night there were new nuances in the music that I never had heard on a previous listening. The Jonathan Tunick orchestrations of the original score were so layered and magnificent that the thrill each night of performing it never eased. There were the complicated quartets, the soaring character songs that Mrs Lovett sang, the conniving characters that set it all in motion, each time thrilling. .

Let's not ignore the complicated subject manner of terror and murder! Not to mention what was done with the bodies. However were it not based upon a true event it could be dismissed more easily. Stephen Sondheim and Hugh Wheeler did not invent this in a vacuum. It truly happened and had been based upon a play about the subject. In an interview during the Sondheim festival in Washington, DC some years ago, Sondheim actually said something very interesting about it. He felt that Sweeney plays today even more effectively because as we now live in a world of terror where ones' personal agenda for revenge can wreak havoc on millions. That is at the core of the Sweeney Todd story.

Yet there is also much musical brilliance. The young ingénue character is viewed differently by four different male characters and each one sings an ode to Johanna that is an individual unique tribute from their perspective. One version is a romantic idyll of love, another heartfelt loss of pain and yet another wicked evil song of perversion. Each with a sense of integrity to the character that sings them not reprises of the same song.

Valerie Perri (who was herself directed by the genius Hal Prince in "Evita") told a story of accompanying Hal Prince to see a matinee of Sweeney on tour. He paced as was his normal but came to sit down next to her when the scene where Pirelli has been "slashed" but is not yet dead and his hand is desperately flaying to get noticed that he is alive and in a trunk. The evil judge has arrived and hopes that the judge will see him and rescue him. During this the song "Pretty Women" where the judge himself might get slashed is sung. The audience will be seeing great suspense. The scene was full of tension and squirming for the audience.

Hal turned to her and said "I can't believe I did that and winced himself"

Sweeney set new standards in place for complicated story telling in a musical and yet although the movie lost much of the dark humor, was relatively authentic to the stage version. It became realistically way too bloody for my taste. On stage it was bloody but not so in your face that you couldn't watch. In the movie one had to really turn away.

It is still a masterwork!

20 Best Musicals since 1980

- *42nd Street*
- *Sunday In the Park With George*
- *Dreamgirls*
- *La Cage Aux Folles*
- *Into the Woods*
- *Lez Miz*
- *The Phantom of the Opera*
- *Passion*
- *The Producers*
- *The Lion King*
- *Beauty and the Beast*
- *Hairspray*
- *Spamalot*
- *Next to Normal*
- *In the Heights*
- *The Drowsy chaperone*
- *Avenue Q*
- *Book of Mormon*
- *Gentleman's Guide to love and Murder*
- *Hamilton*

42nd Street

With "A Chorus Line" giving us a modern day perception of Broadway why not resurrect the original Broadway musical saga form the 1930's? Based upon the movie "42nd Street", the musical is a depression era fable of the great dictatorial director "Julian Marsh" putting on a musical. This captured the nostalgia craze and the current top hit at the time by taking a vantage point of 50 years earlier when a more innocent back stage story was written.

The musical was a triumph and David Merrick, the producer gambled that the nostalgia craze might still be alive and that the interest in seeing a Broadway musical based upon a movie could really work. It was a gamble as the only recent attempt to make a Broadway Musical out of a movie was with a staging of 'GIGI" which was a major disaster and flop.

However, the opening night triumph was overshadowed by tragedy. Following a lengthy standing ovation, Merrick went onstage and stated, "It is tragic...Gower Champion died this afternoon." He went on to explain that Champion had died of cancer just hours before the performance, "when he said that Mr. Champion had died, there were gasps and screams."-The producer had advised only Bramble (a co-author of the musical) of Champion's death and managed to keep the news a secret from the cast and crew, and the public prior to his announcement. The public backlash to the way it was handled and the publicity used to boost the production by Merrick soured people on Merrick and this was his last Broadway success until his death in 2000.

However that aside that fable of the chorus girl being picked to go on and become a star was infectious and a wonderful delight enabling this musical to become the 14th longest running musical in Broadway history.

Gower Champion had created a final masterpiece he never lived to see, and was a needed final triumph for him as he had some serious missteps and flops during the 1970's.

Dreamgirls

Michael Bennet created one last masterpiece and "Dreamgirls" was created in a vision started by Hal Prince in Evita—A nonstop 360 presentation of action that showed the front and backstage action nonstop all of the time.

It was amazing how the girl groups of the 1960's became the catalyst for the musical. Ok it was not really about the

Supremes, but there were hints there that it could be. Michael Bennet's reflection on the Sixties and his years on Hullabaloo (the 60's TV show) gave him real inspiration for this.

Some think this equals "Gypsy" as the greatest showbiz saga ever. That can be debated, but the whirling towers and the continual action certainly created a scene of constant action and continual multi-dimensional storytelling.

The story emphasizes the cross over to white audiences and the costs that took on the black performers who could not adjust to that style. It was not a real transition, but one that seemed needed to make the singers real stars for the audience power. Hence the parallels between the real James Brown and the real Diana Ross that makes the story seem to be aping a reality that truly did not exist.

It also plays out against the civil rights riots in the mid 60's although not to real detail and highlights the result of what happened to a singer who gets thrown away because love interests and career strategy collide.

It too of course became a star making vehicle for Jennifer Hudson in the movie, and "Dreamgirls" was given new life 25 years later as a result.

Yet in the original it was the nonstop motion that Michael Bennet gave to these groups that soared. Yet with it all "Dreamgirls" was about the price of success, yet it also talks about the ideas of black culture assimilating into white America front and center. It was seemingly the tale of selling out to the highest bidder that is never quite forgotten.

It is a milestone for sure—and one to love. If you want a magical experience, listen to it as it was done in concert with Audra Macdonald. It is fantastic!

La Cage Aux Folles

French farce about two long-time partnered gay men and the son they raised was a major breakthrough for a Broadway love story. Yes it was truly PG in Presentation but cleverly crafted and enduring.

Jerry Herman had faded away after the "Mack and Mabel" disaster of the early 1970's and he felt that his version of musical story telling was not the taste of the current era. Traditional book musicals were not really the genre of the day and he felt that. Along came the farce of "LA Cage Aux Folles" and the first ever same sex love story became musical theatre fodder. The scales of the script were balanced between issue and entertainment. Harvey Fierstein who was a vocal gay activist created a story with feel good and message.

It was a daring step at the time, and the score was typical Jerry Herman style. Buoyant, fizzy, and happy made the musical atmosphere work. The Drag chorus was a delight for the audience and it set newly emerging acceptable themes forward.

Sadly the AIDS epidemic arrived at the same time and over the years that followed La Cage fell flat and seemed dated, yet with a period of years passing the fresh approach of the revival raised the awareness once again and demonstrated how good material is still good material.

"La Cage" works because it was tender, real, and recognizable. The anthem, "I Am What I Am "worked because the characters were well fleshed out and not caricatures of people. For the bridge and tunnel crowd to accept the themes and the characters openly there had to be real people on stage who were able to be recognized.

A sad note is that when "La Cage" closed Jerry Herman walked into the street (allegedly) and vowed he had nothing to prove and would never write a Broadway Musical again. That has in fact been the case.

~

Sunday In the Park With George

In the same year as "La Cage" another true original masterpiece was created. "Sunday in the Park with George" deals with the price an artist pays for his gifts. Many choose to believe that the character of Seurat is a riff on Mr. Sondheim himself. A man who as a character has attention to detail and is about doing something different than the peers would consider at the time.

Let's not argue that discussion at all, as I once heard Mr. Sondheim state that critics and others who write of pieces often think they know what was going on in the authors head when a piece gets written, and their ideas are often wrong. Yet the piece is so interesting in terms of how an artist deals with his art that you must stand back and be in awe.

One of the most stirring moments ever in a musical is at the end of Act I when the artist fixes his subjects and each character comes together to build the painting. It is reminiscent of Bernstein musically in "Candide" when the entire cast sings A Capella in "Make Your Garden Grow." Sondheim uses the same A Capella technique and the chills you get for the cast singing "Sunday" and being in permanent position on that painting is an incredible moment. It always creates chills.

The second great moment is when the Second Act opens and the characters in the painting start complaining about being whom and where they are.

Yet the brilliance continues in so many ways. The style of music the Seurat character sings is all staccato representing the dots that Seurat paints. When the second act character connects the dots in his life suddenly he sings in legato phrases so brilliantly conceived by Mr. Sondheim.

The piece is again not driven on plot and there is little if any Choreography but the impact of the "plot" truly resonates with intelligence.

After all It is Sondheim and always groundbreaking and audience challenging.

One odd remembrance, when Jerry Herman 's "La Cage Aux Folles" won best musical over "Sunday In the Park", Mr. Herman in his most ungracious took a slam at Mr. Sondheim saying something to the effect—he said "a simple, hummable tune is still alive on Broadway" and was totally sticking it to Sondheim's pointillism-inspired score for *Sunday in the Park with George*. "Sunday" won the Pulitzer Prize for Drama and Mr. Sondheim won best score.

This all can be seen in a taped live version as done by PBS and available on DVD—truly worth seeing Bernadette Peters and Mandy Patinkin creating these roles.

James Lapine and Stephen Sondheim created a new team. After the collapse of the Sondheim Prince relationship from the "Merrily We Roll Along" disaster, Sondheim and Prince thought they needed a break. Many have said that they exhausted each other; others felt that they needed new vision, but in any event this new partnership created something quite dramatic and unique.

A painting and an artist that had very little actual fact and history became the Pulitzer Prize winning Musical that creates deep questions about artists and what they do for their art. As the song says in the play "art isn't easy".

Bernadette Peters and Mandy Patinkin took on the difficult vocal challenges and were both over the top in the achievement. Sondheim tells the story of committed Patinkin who as he is about to draw the dog into the painting musically has to emulate the sounds of the bark and he come prepared with multiple barking options to choose from.

You listen to Sondheim and suddenly you hear something new, like the brilliance of the way Sondheim used staccato for the pointillist artist until he connected the dots in his own life and then sang legato phrases. It is pure genius in thematic writing. Of course the female girl friend of the artist had to have the name "Dot" as well.

When you love the brilliance of Sondheim it does not really matter. It's all good.

~

The Phantom of the Opera

Once upon a time there was this incredibly anticipated musical directed by Hal Prince and written by Andrew Lloyd Weber and Charles Hart, a classic Beauty and the Beast horror story. It is based upon the classic novel by Leroux.

When a musical has been running for a generation, and has grossed over 5 billion dollars you have to say it is exceptional even if now it has become a bit ho-hum and one wonders who the people are that still goes to see this. When it opened it became a phenomenon, a major attraction and a marketing marvel.

Lloyd Webber's score is sometimes operatic in style but maintains the form and structure of a musical throughout. The full-fledged operatic passages are reserved principally for subsidiary characters such as Andre and Firmin, Carlotta, and Piangi. They are also used to provide the content of the fictional "operas" that are taking place within the show itself. Lloyd Webber used "pastiche" of various styles from the grand operas of Meyerbeer, Mozart, and Puccini. These pieces are often presented as musical fragments, interrupted by dialogue or action sequences in order to clearly define the musical's "show within a show" format. The musical extracts from the Phantom's opera, "Don Juan Triumphant", during the latter stages of the show, are dissonant and modern—"suggesting, perhaps, that the Phantom is ahead of his time artistically.

The other music is of a pop score nature and contrasts directly with the classical sound of the operas that are performed. In some was the structure seems copied from "Kiss Me Kate" in style, the clash between performance and real life.

Oddly enough, many estates of many composers including Puccini claimed that there was plagiarism. Many suits were settled out of court, but Lloyd Weber known for his irascible style just moved onward and did not let this interfere with the great success of the musical.

It of course is a large and dramatic production. The music has become internationally recognizable. None of the music became pop-culture hits, but the musical has been heard by so many that to ignore its accessibility would be churlish.

Its success alone makes it an icon of the lavishness and enormity of the musicals of the era.

~

Into the Woods

As a second outing James Lapine and Steven Sondheim took familiar fairy tales and explored the adult implications of what happens after "happily ever after". It is fascinating to see how the works of Sondheim have become accepted and so mainstream that even Disney now makes Sondheim movies!

The familiar stories "Little Red Riding Hood", "Cinderella", "Rapunzel" among others getting fractured and viewed from an adult perspective yet accessible enough for children .The role of a witch who casts an evil spell on a couple so that they cannot have children, then sending them into the allegorical woods to break the spell is the catalyst of the story.

When it opened in 1987, Frank Rich JR, a great admirer of Mr Sondheim made positive mention of the lyrics naturally, and the music, and made note of the struggle with life and its "adventures." He felt the plot overly long and perhaps even overwhelmed by the need to get songs on for the star Bernadette Peters, yet over time this was the first truly widely accessible musical that Mr .Sondheim had written.

Seeing it a week or two after its 1987 opening was thrilling. Yet remember, Sondheim could have set the phone book to music and I would have loved it. "Children Will Listen" and "No One is Alone" are powerful pieces of music as well the prince's duets "Agony". The score has so many wonderful gems.

Also reflect upon the stories Mr. Sondheim shared how the character of the witch was not based upon his mother as so many decided it had been. To hear him ask "how does a critic or scholar know what the writer was writing about if they had not been told directly by the author" is interesting food for thought! If you listen to the "Sondheim On Sondheim" recording one could make that leap about the witch and his mother but he also has said that the character of the witch was not based upon his interpretation of her at any level.

Overshadowed by the big productions of the time in terms of run, it has been revived often with great casts, Vanessa Williams among them and still is a great evening of theatre. Tell me when it is playing (as with any Sondheim piece—excluding one maybe) and I'm there.

~

Lez Miz

I first saw Lez Miz two weeks after it opened on Broadway and was so far away in the balcony I thought I was across the street, But the sweep of the story the strength of the music was so powerful that even a mile away in the theatre it kept a focus for all of the 3.5 hours it runs.

The story of course is one we all know, and yet it seemed fresh new and exhilarating.

The pop opera style worked and one could be blown away that there were really so many wonderful tenor roles.

It is such a blend of Music, drama, scenery, character and of course "power" that you are overwhelmed and taken over by its shear strength. Seeing all of those people on stage is thrill enough. It's not a big story yet it is told in a big way, almost like the old movies that said "cast of thousands". When"Bring Him Home", is sung, can you really not cry? The duets, quartets, the romance the passion, it's all there.

My favorite Les Miz story however is about Patti Lupone who played the original Fontine in London. After she dies on stage she has about 2/12 hours before she comes back as a ghost at the end. She fell asleep and they couldn't find her. She recants this in her book so I am not making it up.

I was not a total fan of the movie. Broadway imagination sometimes is better than the reality of a movie. Hugh was really terrific but until the second half I was not over the top in love with the whole thing. It is good and the way they did the singing live is amazing, but it's a bit too over the top in so many ways and a little uneven with the choices of actors.

Still it's pretty amazing anyway.

Passion

When Sondheim goes at something he really does. Based upon an Italian movie "Passione d'Amore" this extraordinary unusual beautiful musical is all about love, sex, passion, beauty, power and manipulation. Sondheim conceived this all by himself. Many have thought this is the most romantic piece that Sondheim ever wrote and it is just lush and gorgeous to hear.

Yet in its original run it was considered by many too dark, too emotional and maybe too operatic for its own good.

The idea of a handsome soldier being pursued by a truly ugly woman, inside and out, and how her love for him almost destroys them both was not everyone's taste. The musical opened to glowing reviews but did not find an audience even though it won major award recognition .Clive Barnes gave the musical a rave review, "Once in an extraordinary while, you sit in a theater and your body shivers with the sense and thrill of something so new, so unexpected, that it seems, for those fugitive moments, more like life than art. *Passion* is just plain wonderful — emotional and yes, passionate . . . Sondheim's music — his most expressive yet — glows and glowers, and Tunick has found the precise tonal colorations for its impressionistic moods and emotional overlays. From the start of his career, Sondheim has pushed the parameters of his art. Here is the breakthrough. Exultantly dramatic, this is the most thrilling piece of theater on Broadway".

The public somehow was scared off by the perceived material and became the shortest run of any "Best Musical" winning play. To see this and watch it is an unusual experience as the audience never applauds after a musical section until the end is startling. It just happens over you, sweeping you away until you are totally enraptured.

It was captured on DVD and is worth watching

Beauty and the Beast

It is hard to decide why this is on the list, but frankly it helped reinvent how Broadway Musicals would be created and produced in the future. It was all about the brand and the expansion of a catalogue of cartoons.

Let's face it Disney has a huge catalogue.

It always horrified me to think that I would take my grandchildren to a Disney Musical as their first visit to a Broadway musical. Fortunately that was not the case, but the idea of a non-original cartoon based musical that came to life in theme park fashion was just not the tradition of Broadway that I wanted to impart upon my next generation.

The Disney cartoon was certainly wonderful and who could argue with the voice of Angela Lansbury as a teapot. Yet converting that to live theatre also meant adding to it and filling it out into a two act extravaganza.

It did what it was supposed to do for Disney and the musical theatre in general. It created a brand based musical, one in which the actors would just be "fillers" portraying the brand that they represented. For Disney it was far cheaper that way. No major egos to contend with and the name of the actor was not the idea, it was the piece itself. They have captured brands that way and are having great success. It must be disappointing to the actor looking to break through on the one hand but it does get them paid!

To be on this list as a best is obvious, it would be wrong to omit it. Yet what it did was create the Broadway musical as a tourist attraction like a Circle Line Boat in Manhattan and give the tourist the chance to think they are seeing real theatre. It was always beautiful, the score singable and a unique breakthrough.

It created a new art form, the theme park musical!

The Lion King

If you haven't seen this magnificent piece of musical theater, than you are missing something. The beginning with the animals entering the theatre is so magical and beautiful that even a detractor would wonder what you are complaining about.

OK, so this too is a Disney cartoon made into a full-fledged musical evening, but it is not like"Beauty and the Beast". Julie Taymor created a magical magnificent uniquely different presentation where the animals are actually presented in masks where you forget the human faces that appear.

The story is Hamlet set to Disney and that is expanded from the ever popular cartoon of the same name. . It is still running and truly a magnificent evening of spectacle.

Only the very most jaded would ever hate it. It is still running how many years later and shows no end in sight.

~

The Producers

For my 50th birthday, months in advance when it was first advertised that the musical with Nathan Lane and Matthew Broderick would open on my big event I ordered tickets for my entire family. How could it be anything but fantastic? Knowing the movie well, and the story and those involved how could it possibly miss?

We arrive at the theatre and get our seats. A habit of ours was to look at the program to see if our longtime friend

Peter Marinos might be in it. My wife says after looking at her program "no one we know in it". I look and went nuts as sure enough there was Peter. I summoned the usher sent a note back stage and much to the shock of my ever doubtful sons (oh Dad like he will even remember you!!!), we were invited back stage after the performance to have Peter join us for dinner.

We heard great stories of how Anne Bancroft was really the muse for her husband Mel Brooks, and that she was present everywhere validating for him if something was funny. We heard about Peters' audition where you had to make Mel Brooks laugh. Yet most memorable of all was seeing the excitement a friend had about being a part of something special and so very big. He was a cast member the entire run of the show.

Of course being in the theatre (Peter aside) was spectacular. Seeing a Broadway musical three days after it opens that gets rave, rave, rave reviews sitting there was pretty exciting. Matthew Broderick and Nathan Lane were at their top form and the whole production had an energy that was incredible to watch. This was theatre history being made and soon logged with its record setting Tony wins soon to follow.

"The Producers" also changed the way seats were bought for musicals. It was such a big smash that to get people to pay more for the front rows were priced at a much higher level (like 400.00) and those that had to really get in to see it at any cost were thus accommodated. This practice holds even today in some theatres and has created a huge backlash to some. It did not help "Young Frankenstein" and created a huge arrogant backlash about it.

"The Producers" however which is raunchy, sophisticated borscht belt humor at its best with visual aids to support it is a great musical. How lucky we have it.

Spamalot

Oh the great Mike Nichols! He gave us a comic gem that made no sense, as a salute to the Monty Python style and yet was clever funny. It was a satirical wonder of Broadway and Entertainment.

It is amazing when two satirical arenas collide! To some it was called scrapbook musical theatre where cultural phenomena collide with jukebox musicals and wide fan bases. All of this is a step beyond the Disney mold. In the era of "The Producers" where Broadway and inside jokes were lambasted the same occurs here in "Spamalot".

It is a two level inside joke of sorts. First you have to satisfy the Monty Python people who look for scenes and instantly break into laughter, but the musical side adds a satirical piece to the current style of Broadway and explodes it. Where else could you create a song that says "You can't have Broadway if you don't have any Jews"? or the song "What ever happened to my part?"

What is so wonderful about "Spamalot" is that none of it makes sense; there is not a real plot, as if you would really care for one, and it is a connection of comic antics crafted by the genius that was Mike Nichols.

On the wall of my office is a special artifact from "Spamalot". During the "Broadway Cares" event shortly after the show had opened with the original cast intact, the cast sold the option to get a picture taken with the entire cast. On my wall hangs the picture with Tim Curry, David Hyde Pierce, Hank Azaria, and Sara Ramirez all standing with the Friedman guys. It is something we really cherish and I love having it.

As the song says "Always look on the Bright side if Life".

Hairspray

Recently on a cruise I met Richard Frankels' (the guy who produced Hairspray) brother Steve. He is an avid theatre fan and loved the exchanges we had about the theatre. "Hairspray" is also following the genre of musicals that take a movie or semi familiar movie and rev it up with music to enhance what it was.

The conceit, from the movie was a that a man in drag always played the mother character, and with Harvey Firestein who wrote it, and then assuming the lead it was as over the top as one could imagine. Having lived in the DC / Baltimore area most of my life it is amazing to see the racism of the 1960's played out in this truly unique way with blue collar 1960's humor and music.

It is one of those pieces of modern musical theater that set out to capitalize on the generation that loved "Bye Bye Birdie", "Grease " and "The Producers", taking genre enhancing nostalgia and putting serious themes forward with clever wit and humor.

What this musical did was create old fashioned musical comedy without at all being old fashioned. A character in drag would hardly have been on stage 40 years ago, lets face it.

In fact on the post 9/11 era that this occurred in itself was terrific to know that a musical could still be nice and it really was.

The musical lampooned a serious message about racial integration, using a bygone beloved era to focus the political and cultural impact of the story. It is a love letter to the musicals of the 1950's nostalgia yet at the same time tells a story about differences all humorously and packing a real punch.

The music truly is of its alleged time and wonderfully conceived by Shaiman and Whitman. The script was over the top and pays due homage to the original movie. It ran for over 2500 performances and is a gem of the new millennium where American book musicals finally rose back to the top of the creative heap.

~

In the Heights

Seeing this you could really be thinking how really different this truly was.

The idea of 72 hours in the life a Bodega owner and his neighbors in Washington Heights (A Manhattan Neighborhood) was revealing in terms of life style issues, dreams, realities and in fact a nod toward acceptance, a modern immigrant struggle and racism

The opening number and many others performed in a rap style tell a tale in a new form of musical. It almost goes back to a happier version of "West Side Story" with Latin influenced music, the happier transition of an immigrant population in Manhattan and the life style that they live. One identifies with the aspirations of the girl who chose the wrong school for her future, and the guy who owns the bodega their views of life, as well as the parents of the children they have brought here hoping for something better.

It is the immigrant experience that pleasantly plays out against the micro nation of upper Manhattan. To not love this piece would almost be almost be un-American. In many ways it reminds one of the themes of "Fiddler on the Roof" and the breakdown of traditions. It is also the excitement of a new generation of Broadway composer and his insight into the composition options one can create.

Who knows if it is brilliant? I do know that it was truly enjoyable and wonderful fun, genre bending and uniquely creative.

~

The Drowsy Chaperone

What a gem this was. A spoof of a 1920's musical that came alive in someone's living room that was clever and satirical. The story concerns a middle-aged, asocial musical theatre fan; as he plays the record of his favorite musical, the (fictional) 1928 hit *The Drowsy Chaperone*; the show comes to life onstage around him as he wryly comments on the music, story, and actors and all of the inane plot twists that the genre utilized.

The history of this was that it started as a gift for a stag party for the wedding of Bob Martin a writer and Janet Van Der Graf.

From there and the fringe festival in Toronto it grew into what it became.

The concept that the audience is listening to the musical on an old LP record is used throughout the show. As he listens to the show, Man in Chair is torn between his desire to absorb every moment of the show as it unfolds and his need to insert his personal footnotes and his extensive-but-trivial knowledge of musical performances and actors, as he frequently brings the audience in and out of the fantasy. As the show goes on, more of his personal life is revealed through his musings about the show, until, as the record ends, he is left again alone in his apartment—but still with his record of a long-beloved show to turn to whenever he's blue.

At one point, the record "skips", which causes the last notes (and dance steps) of a song to be repeated until the

Man in Chair can bump the turntable. A “power outage” near the end causes the stage to go dark in the middle of the big production number. Despite the show-within-the-show being a two act musical, *The Drowsy Chaperone* is played without an intermission; at the end of the “show’s first act, the Man in Chair observes that there would be an intermission “if we were sitting in the Morosco theatre watching *The Drowsy Chaperone*. Which we’re not.” (In the original Broadway production, he added, “They tore it down and put up a hotel,” an in-joke reference to the fact that the show was playing in the Marquis Theatre, part of the Marriott Marquis complex built on the spot where the Morosco stood). His monologue at the musical’s intermission point ends when he changes records (ostensibly preparing the turntable to play the musical’s second act), then leaves the stage “to use the bathroom”. The new record is actually the second act of a different musical by the same composer and librettist, starring many of the same actors. *Message from a Nightingale* is performed in costumes evoking Imperial China, with the performers displaying clichéd Chinese accents and mannerisms. The Man in Chair returns to the stage and replaces the disc with the correct one for Act II of *The Drowsy Chaperone.*

The plot incorporates mistaken identities, dream sequences,, an unflappable English butler, an absent-minded dowager, a Broadway impresario and his Follies production, comic gangsters, a ditzy chorine, a harried best man, and Janet’s “Drowsy” (i.e. “tipsy”) Chaperone, played in the show-within-a-show by a blowzy *Grande Dame* of the Stage, specializing in “rousing anthems” and not above upstaging the occasional co-star.

It is so clever that you sit back and simply smile! Terrific and Fun!

~

Avenue Q

If you grew up watching Sesame Street and understood the teaching philosophy (or even if you didn't) the idea of a Sesame Street for adults is priceless and rollicking fun.

The great idea is that each character is a puppet and a puppeteer and after a while one forgets who is who believe it or not. Even though I was not the target market, I was over 12 and still over 40 the performance connects on many levels. It is pure satire of our hopes and ambitions. As a parent I kept wondering where do we go wrong with this generation?

It is the world according to children's television and adult life. Avenue Q is a different sort of musical; it is small, packs a satirical punch and at the same time resonates because the truth is in the satire. You can't miss it.

In fact seeing puppets have sex on stage—was it startling LOL—hardly but this then gave it an R rating for families even though the show had puppets. This is in itself funny!

It is interesting to realize that "Avenue Q" is a coming-of-age parable, addressing and satirizing the issues and anxieties associated with entering adulthood. Its characters lament that as children, they were assured by their parents, and by children's television programs such as that they were "special" and "could do anything"; but as adults, they have discovered to their surprise and dismay that in the real world their options are limited, and they are no more "special" than anyone else. It deals with great coming of age issues, racism, and sexuality, career choices, entering adult life and earning a living.

It is truly charming delightful and powerful in its simple approach. Musicals have really changed.

Next to Normal

Making a musical about the destruction of depression on a family is not exactly light hearted stuff. I recall being really nervous to go and see this. The NY Times reviews that said it is not a feel good musical it a feel everything musical.

The music itself was astonishing as it revealed a tale of deep family woe that caused mental strife and breakdown. Totally being worn down by the true angst the suffering characters were dealing with on stage was mesmerizing and at the same time emotionally overwhelming. At intermission I could not move and after I could not talk for some time. It was shattering. Every single person in the audience knew someone, who had life tragedies that created the sorts of depression that some suffer, yet never had I sat riveted by music to personal angst. It was exhausting and exhilarating.

This is a deeply personal musical even if exhausting. I still recall crying because of how I empathized for a friend who suffered from a depression issue that could not be easily handled. The character onstage in many ways could have been my friend.

When you think of the recent times that have brought revivals, and all of the musicals based upon films, you then feel and see how daring this piece. Yorkey and Kitt created something of such power that it truly becomes clear that a musical can have true depth and feeling to move beyond expectations.

If you have never seen this then you must, if you worry it will hurt, well it may challenge but you will survive the challenge and have understanding and empathy.

Book Of Mormon

People ask me all of the time, what did you think of the" Book Of Mormon" I loved it I was taken by it, I thought it got a bit old but it is wonderful and the salute it give to the Broadway that came before it is inspiring beyond belief.

OK so it is irreverent, tasteless, in your face and certainly not for the faint of heart, but if you can accept all of that nothing is sacred (no puns intended) and it is a laugh you cannot imagine.

The best part is what it does to pay homage to the Broadway musicals that have come before it. The second act story of the church told in the fashion of "Uncle Tom's Cabin" from "The King and I" or the creative nonsense all around that pulls something form one Broadway musical of another.

On the other hand if you are looking for a low key delightful musical entertainment this is not it, but who needs that either. It is a very "smutty" over the top kind hearted story of two young men finding their way. The story has a kind heart which makes it watchable.

In a recent PBS special about Mel Brooks they noted that you would not have the "Book of Mormon" if you had not had "Blazing Saddles" first. It is absurd and pokes fun of what we cherish with robust humor and homage to the stage musicals that has come before.

It too captures a new formula. The show is the brand not the people in it. This is again the beneficiary of the Disney Model that if the show is good enough you do not need names on the marquee, just the name of the show. For the producer it is a lot cheaper that way.

~

Gentleman's Guide to Love and Murder

It is wonderful when you attend a musical and you aren't quite sure you will like it and then it envelopes you fully with its wit, satire, charm, and true clever story telling. It is a sort of a riff on Gilbert and Sullivan with operetta style musical and style.

Oddly enough, if you listen to it up front it is a bit off putting as it is so operetta like that you wonder what is in fact going on. Yet the conceit of a long lost far removed heir seeking to reclaim his title by murdering all of those ahead of him in line is pretty nuts as it goes and the complications and double entendre that exists often in the musical lyrics is pretty magical.

What makes this special is that is reminiscent of an earlier style yet at the same time is very contemporary and clever. It is rooted in the early 1900's Edwardian England, yet chooses to embrace a style that emulates a period but could never have been written then, It is way to "outré" for that and is far too sophisticated aping its source.

It is a great time and no one should be put off by what they perceive the evening to be, it is far better than one can imagine. It is clever, funny, outrageous and true social satire.

~

Hamilton

It is still a leap to think that the Charnow biography of Alexander Hamilton hit Lin-Manuel Miranda in the head and launched the idea for a pop rock hip hop pop opera of the founding father we know the least about.

Being among the lucky first to have seen it let's face it this was hard to imagine going in. "The New York Times" review that started with "yes it really is that good" sums it up.

This is musical that will be the "Okahoma!", or "A Chorus Line of this era. It will change the Broadway story telling experience. It is not just that the actors are ethnic portraying the founding fathers (after all in "the King and I" "Siamese" portrayed the south of Uncle Tom's cabin and it was believable) or that the story is highly complex (see Lez MIZ). It is that a story is being told so creatively, so focused on events, the music and the character in a historically accurate way that this is mind blowing.

How a story gets told to music has been a recent evolution in the musical theatre. Some have proclaimed that the Broadway musical is a relic of years ago that somehow still keeps at it. Yet the style of "Hamilton" is not new, the musical story telling certainly is, but that is all a part of the conceit of the story.

To think you can go into theatre and be mesmerized today by a musicalized portrayal of our history is a stunning feat. As this is being written the recording has just hit the market. Having listened again, yes there were times in the theatre I had hoped for super titles to catch all of the words, yet the recording gives a depth to what was present on stage that is even more incredible.

Somethings are too amazing for words. This is one. It seems to be becoming a new phenomenon.

The 16 Best Revivals Ever

- ☆ *Chicago 1996*
- ☆ *Annie Get Your Gun 1966 (Ethel Merman)*
- ☆ *Sweeney Todd (John Doyle) 2005*
- ☆ *Company (John Doyle) 2006*
- ☆ *No No Nanette 1971*
- ☆ *South Pacific (Bartlett Sher) 2008*
- ☆ *Follies 2011*
- ☆ *Gypsy 1973, (Bernadette) 2003 and (Patti) 2008*
- ☆ *Candide 1974*
- ☆ *Kiss Me Kate 1999*
- ☆ *A Little Night Music 2009*
- ☆ *Guys and Dolls 1992*
- ☆ *Porgy and Bess 2012*
- ☆ *Carousel 1994*
- ☆ *La Cage Aux Folles 2010*
- ☆ *On The Town 2014*

Chicago!

After the original fought to run, with Gwen Verdon and Chita Rivera appearing on every television show you can imagine hyping their new musical, the cynical book and style just was not a match for the time. The original recording on Arista records had even gone out of print and you could not get one other than at that one very expensive record store in Times Square that had it for over $100.00.

Musicals often appear in their time and are a victim of the era they appear in. "A Chorus Line" was the new kid in the block also and overshadowed "Chicago", not to mention that most reviewers at the time just did not buy the idea of the news media influencing trials and justice.

It was cynical and frosty. The Fosse choreography and the way the story was told seemed way to off-putting to be real.

Time has a way of changing our outlook on things. The OJ Simpson trial and the media frenzy it created certainly had its ability to get a few folks to re-examine Chicago. Anne Reinking, a fosse Protégé was willing to stage it for the City Center of New York in their Encores series and lucky me I happened to be in town and saw the opening night. It was fantastic.

The reviews of the City Center event were phenomenal and suddenly Bebe Neuwirth and Anne Reinking had positioned themselves well as the faded /murderesses of the story.

They, in many ways, modeled their style after Chita Rivera and Gwen Verdon and if you have seen clips of the two originals it is hard to imagine anyone better, but frankly the revival cast new images of what Chicago can be.

"Chicago" now has been through its re-imagined self has become the longest running American musical ever, and some 18 years later still has energy and phizz. I personally still sing the "Cell Block Tango" and my wife and I Still joke about how Amos made love to Roxy, like he was fixing a carburetor.

Chicago also reinvented the movie musical, with Rob Marshall imagining it anew. We owe so much to this revival that to not be included on this list would be a mistake.

Annie Get Your Gun Lincoln Center 1965

The reputation of this revival was "Granny Get Your Gun" but having never seen Ethel Merman live, as a fourteen year old, being taken to see her do her Ethel thing was an amazing thing to witness. She could blast out the balcony and I loved seeing it. In fact other than the movie, seeing "Annie Get Your Gun" was a rare occurrence.

This was all about preserving Ethel and Annie as a shrine. Lincoln Center really did it and it was fun, joyous and the recording was on my top ten lists for a long time. Irving Berlin wrote a new song, 'Old Fashioned Wedding" it was really what musicals were supposed to be weren't they? Wonderful character star based entertainments?

The book was revised to leave out a secondary love story and the book became cleaner, with a sharper feel, it also highlighted Ethel a whole lot more which surely made her very happy. Having seen the awful Betty Hutton movie, seeing this in the flesh was really thrilling.

The new Irving Berlin duet that mimicked the style he wrote in "Call Me Madam", two songs in counterpoint created a new standard "Old Fashioned Wedding".

So the detractors could say she was way too old to play the part, but it wasn't about character anyway. It was about seeing Ethel re-creating one of her great roles even if it seemed far-fetched! Go get the recording and hear what was on that stage! It was terrific (and by the way Jerry Ohrbach was in it too).

~

Sweeney Todd (John Doyle)

Being a "Sweeney Todd" lover and also a fan of the Jonathan Tunick orchestrations it was almost impossible to imagine how a spare presentation where the actors would play their own instruments would even play out. Being used to the over the top large 'Sweeney" with its large cast two level set and the industrial background of the Hal Prince original, it was hard to imagine anything different.

So hearing that John Doyle had re-envisioned Sweeney into a smaller production, where the idea is that it is set in an asylum was hard to imagine.Yet, a new version of a great masterpiece can really work. Invention, can be amazing, to see that a musical could work in a totally different presentation and become even more relevant.

The original that had humor, as dark as it was, still had humor. This new version did not show victims coming to be killed; rather this production used puppets still even more horrifying as the victims seemed so less real and even more terrifying—the victims of a true terrorist. They had no faces. In fact the terror of "Sweeney Todd" seemed far more horrible as the intensity of the actors carrying their own instruments was courageously more differently dramatic.

As a musician myself I could not imagine having to memorize a score, play an instrument and act at the same time. That is one heap of expected talents! Then I wondered how they even found understudies. The production gimmick and all was a marvel and special.

This proves that serious rethinking can get great results. Who knew Patti Lupone could play a tuba, and that Michael Cerveris played the guitar.

~

Company (John Doyle)

After rethinking "Sweeney Todd" John Doyle gave "Company" the same treatment. It was fascinating that the character that facilitates the story, Bobby was cast as a loner outside of the "band" of his married friends. The rest of the cast played their instruments all of the way through.

The original had a distant remoteness to Bobby, as he viewed the relationships of his married friends and observed their relationships. New York was used as a backdrop and allegory of loneliness.

Loving once again the wonderful Jonathan Tunick orchestrations hearing this again with actors playing their own musical instruments changed the sound of the piece and made it obvious smaller and more personal. Bobby was clearly outside of the band until the very end when he sat down at the piano and suddenly played his own piece 'Being Alive" to be joined by the entire cast musically.

If you wonder what this can possibly be like, PBS recorded the production some years ago it captures the performance of Raul Esparza as Bobby, in an icy neutral observation mode.

Having seen "Company" many times over the 40+ years of its existence this was a new glimpse at an old entertaining friend.

~

No No Nanette (1972)

The hippie era was producing 'Hair", and other rock musicals were the norm, be it "Jesus Christ Super Star", "Two Gentlemen of Verona" (a tony winner) or "Godspell". Who would have guessed that an antique, silly inane 1920's musical would get great reviews and get audiences in the theatre. The original music was included and some others pieces included, but the nonsensical plot remained. You also would never have imagined that the average theatre goer at the time would know who Ruby Keeler, Patsy Kelly even were, as they had been hallmarks of the 1930's musical era. Yet sure enough this musical with the hits songs "I Want to Be Happy" and "Tea For a Two" with a Ruby Keeler tap dance would attract wide audiences.

So what is the big deal? This revival created an entire

genre, the major revival with a huge budget, marketing campaign and major names and stars to get people into the theatre.

~

South Pacific 2008 Bartlett Sherr Director

Some years ago, Stephen Sondheim mentioned in an interview that "South Pacific" may be the most problematic of all of the musicals Rodgers and Hammerstein wrote for today's audiences. One could take exception as there are a few others of theirs that are more problematic, "Allegro" for sure being one of them or "Flower Drum Song" being another.

His point being that the attitudes and feelings presented that are exactly connected to a time and place ask the audience to accept the smaller world thinking that is "South Pacific". In its day it was shocking to think Emile was so much older than Nellie, a murderer perhaps, and having children from an earlier marriage to a native woman. Add to that the idleness of sea bees on an island in World War II waiting for the war; most of us do not recall the feelings of those times. Then you had the controversy of Lt. Cable being bare chested holding a native girl after an obvious sexual encounter and was 'You've Got To Be Carefully Taught" really so dramatic today?

Believing in the material, trustfully and casting it to perfection you create a success for a new generation to admire and enjoy. Lincoln Center and Bartlett Sherr decided not to in any way monkey with the original material and insisted that it be staged in the format of the original.

We all know how it ends and I that when Emile returns my entire family sat there with tears rolling down our cheeks. It was just terrific, and one can only imagine how the 1949 audience felt when they saw the musical for the first time.

You felt the longing in Emile, the naiveté of Nellie, the optimism in Lt. Cable and the humorous wickedness of Blood Mary. This demonstrates that Rodgers and Hammerstein truly created masterpieces. This plays today with a freshness that is not expected.

~

Follies

Sondheim lovers have lived for a "Follies" revival for 40+ years and have hoped and hoped it would be a good one. The Kennedy Center put its best foot forward and sure enough they cast a brilliant revival featuring Bernadette Peters as Sally and Jan Maxwell as Phyllis. Usually there are complaints about the book, or the fact that the first act moves along with glib one-liners and dull inane repartee that does not match the lyrics Sondheim wrote until you get to the excitement of the second act, but this time it was magical.

From the opening strains of " Beautiful Girls" to the wonderful pastiche numbers like "Broadway Baby", "Who's That Woman", you were just enraptured by the wonderful Sondheim score and reveled in another Sondheim masterpiece. Enjoying the score, makes the whole piece exuberant and watching a legendary musical get a first class treatment was truly special.

The "Follies" story of how it has become such a cult classic and further explained in the terrific book by Ted Chapin about his experiences while assisting on the original clarify how this truly special and dynamic musical about lost hopes and dreams is far more than the cliché that the reviews at the time thought it might be. In its original production it seemed to be going after the nostalgia craze, but over time that has become clear that craze as not the case at all.

The incredibly wonderful score, with the new recording that adds set up dialogue even clarifies the story for those that wondered about what it was about. Truly a concept musical, not a linear book story line at all it is clear to see how this confused people in 1971. This genre was still new and not widely understood in the post "Hair" era of Broadway musicals.

One keeps hoping for a "Follies" movie with Diane Keaton and Bette Midler not to mention everybody else that the movie would have to have but it would be dream movie come true for many.

The new recording is terrific and well worth having.

~

Gypsy 1973
Angela Lansbury, Bernadette Peters, Patty Lupone

After Ethel Merman put her touch on "Gypsy" in 1959 it was believed that no one could touch the role on stage with any sort of credibility. It took a long time especially after the movie (which disappointed the creators as all of the major players were dubbed) to find someone who was willing to tackle the role.

In 1973 London there had never been a production of 'Gypsy" and Elaine Stritch had been signed but to her dismay tickets were not selling so she was taken off the production to be replaced by Angela Lansbury who fresh from two Jerry Herman vehicles was only too ready to tackle what has been labeled the greatest role ever written for a woman in a musical. Her style and interpretation created a new vision of the role. She wasn't the brash harsh Merman at all but something quite different.

Her performance transferred to Washington DC (the Kennedy Center) and then to Broadway creating a new characterization of Mama Rose, and the result was it led to three other major revivals later on. Each was unique, the Tyne Daly, "Gypsy"; the Sam Mendes, Bernadette Peters, "Gypsy"; and then finally the Patti Lupone "Gypsy".

Each was unique in style and flourish but the last two seem to be the most interesting of all of the Gypsy revivals in recent years. These two have the two strongest leading ladies of the era and putting them both in very different versions of the great warhorse.

Bernadette played the part with sex appeal that had never really existed in the role. After all the character had many men in her life and there must have been a reason.

Arthur Laurents had final approval of anyone who played the role in a Broadway house and rumors flew that he had a feud going with Patti Lupone who truly wanted to play the part in New York. She played it elsewhere but not on Broadway.

"City Center Encores" presented a Gypsy with her as it was not considered a Broadway Production. After seeing her in this production Arthur Laurents relented and she did open a "Gypsy" on Broadway on 2008, only to be closed by the financial disaster that occurred that fall. In some ways it may have been too soon for another "Gypsy" revival but hearing Patti on the recording and Bernadette on hers there are two vastly different characters being created. Two different actresses, one part, two visions!

I'm a "Gypsy" fan and it is in my top ten. Each recording is a treasure. If it weren't for Angela we wouldn't have all of the others.

~

Candide 1974

In 1956, when "Candide" premiered it was a masterpiece musically but a muddle dramatically. It languished for years and never had any major productions but the music was often played in pop concerts and had become a great pride of many symphony repertories.

In the early 1970's the hippie/rock musicals were gaining some popularity. Hal Prince, Stephen Sondheim and Hugh Wheeler looked at the book, using an environmental staging in a huge theatre that would appeal to a new sort of theatre goer. After all, the hero Candide, at least thematically sure was consistent with the antiwar hippie thinking at the time.

It was so wonderfully reimagined in the non-proscenium environment, rollicking all over the large theater space. This truly gave "Candide" a new life. Having seen this version many times and even a newer version, I prefer this version the most. It has been filmed by PBS with Kristin Chenowith and Patti Lupone in Concert; it's a lot of fun and worth watching. The music itself is thrilling, wonderful and the light spirit and energy make it what Bernstein must have intended.

~

Kiss Me Kate 1999

It had been 50 years since "Kiss Me Kate" had been given the real Broadway treatment. Many thought the original book was dated and very passé, but with some tinkering that was ultimately allowed "Kiss Me Kate" was re-worked somewhat for a new generation of theatre goers. This too was filmed for PBS with Rachel York and Brian Stokes Mitchell.

You forget how wonderful this musical is and the strength of what Cole Porter and the Spivaks clever use of the Shakespeare. You could follow the plot of "Shrew" and at the same time see the play within the play work while in the backstage dramatics of the actors see the very similar basis of what Shakespeare created. Some of the plot in the backstage portion is truly vaudeville like, but it still works.

Of course the music was absolutely wonderful, Cole Porter's most sophisticated score the double entendre that are so much his style in full evidence. That famous front of the curtain song 'Brush Up Your Shakespeare" created the multiple encores people expected and became an instant classic.

Some musicals are just plain wonderful based upon when they were written. It's interesting how actresses turn things down and one wonders how Mary Martin turned it down. I can't imagine her in the part at all, but someone did. It required a true diva like character and she didn't match that.

An interesting feat of casting was that Brian Stokes Mitchell played color blind and he and Marin Mazzie certainly commanded the stage and the two couples with so much gusto and verve that the bickering couples work!

Seeing great works with big casts is something we have to cherish as too many great pieces of theatre will be lost based upon sheer size alone.

~

A Little Night Music

For Sondheim fans everywhere, we had all yearned for a great Broadway revival of one of our very dear favorites. The idea of a revival of this perfect musical had been a dream of it's' fans forever and forty years was just too long to wait. Yet it finally happened.

The good news and bad news was that the musical

interpretation of the piece with smaller orchestration was far too slow in tempo and almost killed it. It had been called "lugubrious" by the "New York Times" but seeing it twice, once with Catherine Zeta Jones and Angela Lansbury and then later with Bernadette Peters and Elaine Stritch was purely wonderful and the 4 stars made the musical different.

Elaine was too far gone mentally to be really wonderful. She had to call off stage "Mary—line"—and every time she was on stage you could sense the audience nervous for her. It was Elaine Stritch playing Madame Armfeldt as Elaine Stritch, but she was such an icon you rooted for her. Bernadette was the most wonderful Desiree, ever, and she comes across ageless on stage and her "Send in the Clowns" was a tear jerker if ever there was one. No one has ever done it better—you can pull it up on "YouTube"

Angela Lansbury on the other hand was far more wonderful as Madame Armfeldt and what a shame the original casting wasn't Bernadette and Angela but seeing both casts was still a great event.

The 1973 original cast recording over the newer one is still the best recording, but the newer one has dialogue and storytelling that the original does not have, and the original orchestrations are far better and fuller which was what the piece needs. The lushness of those Jonathan Tunick orchestrations is part of the magic.

As noted earlier,this ranks up there with the perfect musical list, it's a gem.

~

Guys and Dolls 1992

It was never my favorite. I thought the book was slow and clunky and the movie was just awful (Marlon Brando, are you kidding me?) But then again I had never seen a really good production of "Guys and Dolls". The music of course was well known and I loved it but I thought it to be dull and boring just the same.

The 1992 revival changed all of that! It had pitch perfect casting and made stars of three people, Nathan Lane, Peter Gallagher and Faith Prince. It was so iconic that even Woody Allen paid homage to it in his movie "Manhattan Murder Mysteries" as his character and Diane Keaton's character attended a performance during the course of the movie.

So there it was—something exciting and new to fall in love with. It was really perfect. The 1992 recording is a big improvement over the original 1951 recording.

It was also timing. The "American" musical was not doing well at the time as so much talent had evaporated form the AIDS crisis and the big British blockbuster seemed to be the taste of the era. The book musical in its' traditional form seemed destined to be in big over the top glossy versions. Yet suddenly in this era, a well-regarded Broadway revival became once again a major hit. It worked anew.

"Guys and Dolls" is an American masterpiece about of course the imagined Times Square envisioned by Abe Burrows and Frank Loesser based upon the Damon Runyon Stories. Forty years after it had opened it was alive and kicking and a great revival can certainly make an old warhorse of a musical come to life! It is now a favorite!

~

Porgy and Bess 2012

The Gershwin estate has a challenge in that "Porgy and Bess is a well-regarded masterpiece but it is so big and demanding that to stage it requires a major fortune and commitment.

The American Reparatory Theater in Boston approached the Gershwin estate with the idea of reducing the book, editing down the score and creating a more manageable "Porgy and Bess". It starred the wonderful Audra Macdonald and Norm Lewis and the production created a tremendous stir.

It was not a "Porgy and Bess" for purists. It edited out whole sections of music and book, changed the approach, and to some critics just dumbed it down way too much. Stephen Sondheim even wrote a letter to the editor of the Sunday Arts and Leisure section of the NY Times about his dismay that artists could tinker with such a masterpiece. The letter chastised all involved and made it clear that this sort of thing was just horrible from his vantage point.

However, even with fair to rave reviews, there is an excitement about this as " Porgy and Bess " is now able to be handled at a reasonable level and gives smaller groups a version to utilize that does not make it must an undoable piece of work. OK, let's be fair it may not really satisfy the purists out there, but a smaller "Porgy and Bess" is better than no "Porgy and Bess" and how lucky are we be able to have an option available to make it far more visible to audiences.

~

Carousel (1994)

Lincoln Center was very brave with this revival of Carousel.

It was truly dark and they went for color blind casting. This somewhat manipulates the Rodgers and Hammerstein message of classism in New England and because of the color blind casting the resonance of that issue is somewhat misplaced but the story with its' tragic undertones and misguided judgements and relationships was still very powerful.

Added to the mix was a young, Audra Macdonald, who

was dazzling as Carrie Pipperedge, the second female lead and her portrayal of an upwardly mobile friend in the industrial age of New England was exciting. In fact Barbara Cook has even said in concert that this is the far more fun role to play than the lead role Julie Jordan the lead that has tragic events to contend with.

The direction went back to the original approach and took head on that Billy Bigelow was a loathsome character and in fact did not accidentally fall on his knife as is so often portrayed but rather committed suicide out of fear of being caught as a thief and going to jail. This emphasized the ostracizing of his daughter form the kids in her town even further. The sins of the father being transferred to the children, being an important message in the story this becomes even more evident.

"Carousel" was noted to be Richard Rodgers' favorite musical and with its deep complex musical themes, the unique bench scene and the soliloquy one can see why that is. "Carousel" is truly operatic in form, even though it is a musical, but it still created plenty of tears to flow and in this revival was a wonderful re-creation of something special.

~

La Cage Aux Folles 2010

In the 1980's frothy different "La Cage Aux Folles" was an old fashioned musical with a twist—a gay couple at its center. The AIDS crisis moved it to the sidelines and over the next twenty years was looked at as almost a period piece that was cute and fun at its time but just a bit tired in its vision of humor and fun.

A few years before this revival there was an attempt at a full blown, big time revival of the original and it had fair to mild reviews and was viewed almost as a period piece. The casting of Robert Goulet was substituted and that did not help at all. It just seemed past its' prime.

However, the 2008 London revival that was minimalist in approach, almost seedy in its' appearance and without all of the glitzy shine of the original somehow changed the feel of the book. Going to see it out of curiosity as it starred Kelsey Grammar, the attitude chosen going in was this was going to be terrible and that it might get a hoot out of how dated and awful it would be. Nothing could have been further form the reality. Across the aisle sat the author, Harvey Firestein who really laughed out loud at his own jokes but that did not deter anyone from discovering it again. It was a terrific piece being handled in great humor and wit.

Having seen the New York original, remembering it with less than great enthusiasm, never thinking it a great piece of musical theater that had to be revisited, this was a surprise. Yet the smaller, softer version emphasized the relationship of the two men and certainly positioned the romantic issues at hand far more beautifully than the earlier vision of it.

Seeing it again demonstrates the impact dead on perfect casting that made it work. Yes Douglas Hodge the Original London Albin, was wonderful, and as was Kelsey Grammer, but the whole story took shape as both a farce and a softer more visible believable love story. Maybe time had not discarded the story but had in fact enhanced it. In fact it was endearing.

~

On The Town 2014

How is it possible that a 70 year old musical could seem to be written today and that is was about an earlier time rather than being about the time it was written in. The recent John Rando revival was so energetic, and so charismatic that it was hard to believe that it was not a new piece but truly a semi often revived gem form Leonard Bernstein and Comden and Green.

The emphasis on the real steamy hot sexuality the piece has written into it was exciting, and the revival joyously became clever to watch. The ballet sequences (and there are many of them as this was a musical that blended ballet, book and music) were astonishing. The pas de due between Gabey and Ivy (a dream ballet) was so magnificent it stopped the show for a good five minutes with applause.

Striking was the realization of the triple threat requirement for actors today, singing, acting and dancing, but this was not dancing this was ballet and the dancing soared, as did the overall energy of a cast that understood the comedy of the book, the satire, the ultimate sadness yet the buoyancy of a day and what New York added both realistically and symbolically to the characters.

Most wonderful was the full comic realization of the script as well as the blended ballet sequences that matched in energy and scope.

Having seen this piece many times over years it was now as if it had never been seen before and was a fresh new piece of work.

12 Best Opening Numbers in a Broadway Musical

Stephen Sondheim has said in many lectures that the best thing you can do is have a great opening number and if you do have one you can fool and audience for at least 45 minutes before they realize they hate the show.

Recalling that very event occurring was in a musical called "Goodtime Charley" with Joel Gray and Ann Reinking. The opening was great and then about 45 minutes later, it had worn off and the audience being bored to tears. Let's fully agree with Sondheim, and who would want to disagree that he was wrong.

Many people have their favorites, and here's my list!

- ☆ *Comedy Tonight (Forum)*
- ☆ *Prologue (West Side Story)*
- ☆ *Carousel Waltz (Carousel)*
- ☆ *Tradition (Fiddler)*
- ☆ *A Chorus Line (I hope I get it)*
- ☆ *All That Jazz (Chicago)*
- ☆ *Hello (Book of Mormon)*
- ☆ *Wilkommen (Cabaret)*
- ☆ *Fugue for Tinhorns (Guys and Dolls)*
- ☆ *Another Openin' Another Show (Kiss Me Kate)*
- ☆ *Try To Remember (The Fantasticks)*
- ☆ *Rock Island (The Music Man)*

Comedy Tonight (Forum)

If you have heard the recording of "Sondheim on Sondheim" you have heard the master himself tell the story of how this wonderful number came about.

"A Funny thing Happened on the Way to the Forum" had opened in Washington to pretty dismal reviews and George Abbott decided that he better call in a master so Jerome Robbins was sent for.

The number in place to open the show as called "Love is in the Air". In fact if you have seen the movie "The Birdcage" it is sung by Robin Williams and Christine Baranski in a scene in her office as they reminisce about how they met.

Yet, in the opening moments of Forum using that song misled the audience terribly and the audiences did not understand that what they were in for was an evening of robust humor, burlesque style farce and low brow humor crazy antics and comedy. Sondheim went back to the drawing board and was urged to write a new song that would specifically tell the audience what to expect and Jerome Robbins then choreographed a masterpiece of a number visually enhancing the music and words that the audience heard with low brow burlesques style choreography, the rest is history.

It is an opening comic tour de force and masterpiece.

~

Prologue (West Side Story)

Most musicals in this era had voluptuous overtures that warmed the audience up to be prepared to watch the musical that would follow. Overtures were used to first quiet the audience down, but second to introduce music that the audience would hear later on.

In "West Side Story" that idea was abandoned totally as the idea of introducing in a ballet format the visualization of two gangs at war needed to be handled and the opening of "West Side Story" became a ballet of increasing anger and violence that set up the anger of the two gangs that would impact the two young lovers so sadly in the story to come. You don't see good guys or bad guys but you see two sets of very different people colliding in spirit and energy through dance.

The idea was not totally new as certainly in "Carousel" the technique was used instead of an overture, yet Jerome Robbins took it even further.

The concept worked and Jerome Robbins created a magical start to a truly different sort of Broadway musical. The prologue in "West Side Story" allowed Bernstein to project without dialogue, using dance instead as the communication vehicle providing a direct understanding of what the audience would see. Dance and music become connected to deliver the powerful punch that is "West Side Story".

The audience sees the energy of these two gangs, their biased hatred of each other and sense of the pending doom that follows. The tone gets set, brilliantly and with great drama.

~

Carousel Waltz

In 1946 audiences were awaiting an overture and even though Rodgers and Hammerstein had changed openings of musicals by having Curly sing a simple ballad in "Oklahoma" traditional big cast opening scenes were still the norm.

In "Carousel" Agnes De Mille took her ballet style and created an opening that told the story, introduced the characters and did it all in an opening ballet sequence that was melodic and truly beautiful. This musical suite introduced you to all of the characters, gave a foreboding with its minor key and set the tone for the story that would follow. It is a truly beautiful piece of music and dance that separates "Carousel" from other musicals of the time.

You do see early on the womanizing hero, his relationship with his boss, his casual flirtatious approach to women and his carefree amoral attitudes early on. You also see in ballet the reserved nature of his soon to be bride Julie Jordan and her friends. It is a beautiful start to such a sad beautiful story.

~

Tradition (Fiddler on the Roof)

As noted on the discussion of an earlier list, when Bock and Harnick were writing "Fiddler" the focus was originally on the daughters and there was much discussion and disagreement about how to open the musical. Having 5 daughters was not exactly a curse but it was not what most men in small villages had hoped for.

There were many loud sessions among the creative team and finally in a session with Jerome Robbins in frustration Bock or Harnick yelled out something to the effect that the musical was about the breakdown of "traditions" in this community and the impact on Tevye! That created a firmer direction.

They then set out to write an opening that would introduce you to the entire town, the men and their focus, the women and their roles. There were other characters that lived in the town and you learned of their roles, such as Yente the "Matchmaker", the squabbles the villagers have in the community and so forth. In a matter of minutes you learned all you needed to know about this fictional Russian Village. It was rousing, stirring emotional and above all the audience gets invested in the characters they are about to learn more about.

Whenever I see 'Fiddler", (even my granddaughters' school production), the number works and creates a stir and emotion. It is one of the best!

~

A Chorus Line (I hope I get it)

The overture, as a warm up is becoming a relic. The lights come down and boom the play starts. Most of the recent musical hits no longer had them and 'A Chorus Line" is another example.

In the opening of "A Chorus Line" how do you convey the angst, the hope? The fear, the ego and the willingness to do anything to succeed and get cast in a role of a Broadway musical is symbolic to real life. The faces on the pictures, the cruelty of being expected to be able to dance complicated steps you have only seen once, the ability to glow and be special.

In reality the speed and execution of that first number is not so farfetched from the real audition but the psycho-babble would never have been possible with the time constraints of a real audition. Yet within minutes you get a jittery edge as to who will make it and who won't. You see the impact and urgency these auditioning chorus people have and the brash cruelty of the director. It is all there and it fits.

Yet, in those opening minutes in 'A Chorus Line", gives you all of their angst and more; the "strains of I hope I get it?" "How many people does he need?" tells it all.

The universality of "A Chorus Line" is that we all in our own ways perform daily and we put ourselves in the line. This opening affirms what we all do every minute of every day. The fears the hopes the dreams, the anxieties are firmly implanted in those magical opening moments.

~

All That Jazz (Chicago)

Cynicism can really be important to demonstrate right up front. Again no more overtures, just the opening number.

In "Chicago" there had to be an opening number that would set up the whole evenings premise, that murder and other famous trials are tried in the media, and that raw emotion, anger, and public reactions can be carried too far. Look at Nancy Grace for example!

At the beginning moments you are not quite sure who the character is who is singing this number but you wittiness a murder and hear commentary about it all the while by being dazzled by a great example of choreography that is classic. It is story telling mixed to music, it sets an era and a tone.

What is so wonderful about "All that Jazz" is that it talks about an era; it tells the story of murderesses and the crimes they committed with sly over the top humor. The song sets the stage for the vaudeville like story telling that was about appear presenting the corruption of the media and the justice system. Its' is truly just a great song start to finish. You can't help but love it as it sets up the whole premise of Chicago!

~

Hello (Book Of Mormon)

In some musicals satire starts right at the beginning. A whole stage full of Mormon missionaries dressed in their short sleeve white shirts and dark ties ringing doorbells and asking people if they want to read a book about Jesus is so comically satirical and over the top, and in your face that you can't forget the humor, the way religion is mimicked and how we start to laugh at two young guys off to gain their chops converting people for their church.

The humor poked at the serious style of the church is truly outrageous and to this day when we hear a doorbell and hear hello we laugh out loud. It is a great set up and makes the "Book of Mormon" really work. The satire is framed instantly.

From the start you gather the irreverent time you will spend learning about these missionaries and their particular slice of religion. The song "Hello", which has characters interrupting others in comic fashion with lyrics over each other's lyrics that they are hysterical and sets the tone for the rambunctious, raucous material that, will follow.

This is a terrific example of a successful musical number opening. It is clear what the tone is and what is ahead. In fact it almost copies the style of "Comedy tonight" from Forum.

~

Wilkommen (Cabaret)

How do you create creepy, evil, amorality with subtlety and ingenuity in one opening number?

"Cabaret" has to in the opening minutes demonstrate that a world in decline is about to be presented and that people will be complicit with the willingness to accept the decay of morality as a culturally acceptable option.

The character of the MC must at once present himself to the audience as being enticing and welcoming yet at the same time create a skepticism and creepiness so that the audience will always know that when he is present his purpose is to no good end. "Wilkomen" makes that trick happen.

As a member of the audience you are delightfully engaged, misled appropriately and then eerily misjudge what you are seeing. The song is to welcome, but is it really what it is about? Is it a welcome to what? This is an enticement to a decaying society and you will be the complicit witness.

It is a welcome to decay, misery and societal breakdown.

Kander and Ebb set that tone that "Cabaret" would be an evening of disillusionment and the breakdown of a society, leaving the audience stunned and perhaps perplexed at what they have witnessed. In any event that audience is warned to be on edge and by the end of the evening the welcoming song when sung at the end asks "where are your worries now?"

It is theatrical, mood setting and a tour de force for the actor. Again following the recent new style of the non-existent overtures this piece becomes the welcome piece for the audience who is as yet perhaps unknowing of the events that will follow.

~

Fugue for Tinhorns

How do you create a cartoon atmosphere that will lead to stilted purposeful dialogue yet create a mood instantly that will show the audience in a heartbeat two different approaches to a population that exists side by side yet in a neighborhood? These parallel universes become instantly evident in "Guys and Dolls". When you hear the trumpets echoing the starting line of a horse race and hear the strains of "I got the horse right here"—being joined by two others in fugue style you know you are in for a riotous and very different style of musical.

A fugue about horses and a race track about betting then echoed by the singing of the Salvation Army is how you do it. These moments also created the atmosphere of contrasts of these made up inhabitants in a made up semi real place. This pure genius musically clever in its contrasts sets the tone for the characters that will follow all during the performance.

It is then echoed by the Salvation Army singing about saving souls as a deep contrast to the frivolity of the gambler. The conflict of divergent satirical "moralities" is at the center of "Guys and Dolls". It is a terrific piece of composition.

~

Another Openin' Another Show

Cole Porter was a master wordsmith and wanted to demonstrate the pressure of what Broadway openings are all about.

It is exciting and tedious all at the same time. It talked about the angst of a new project, will it make it, or will it close out of town. Will the actors continue to get paid? The lyrics tell it all about the angst and pressure of the actor. It shed slight on the energy it takes to open and yet the fear it takes as well. This just sets the tone and explains the life of an actor.

The song is pure energy, and if you think about the opening of "A Chorus Line" written thirty years later you can sense the angst the actors have giving birth to their roles and their own anxieties.

The audience shares the hopes and dreams and creating a vibrant dream together.

~

Try To Remember

You have to love music with lyrics that uses allegorical reference to set up an evening of fantasy. "Try to Remember, the kind of September when life was slow and oh so mellow". Why September, is life slow in September, usually not ever so that says something—"Try to remember the kind of September when grass was green and grain was yellow, try to remember the kind of September when you were a young and callow fellow".

A simple solo that asks for recall, so one can identify with immature love, long ago memories, the dreams we all have. The beauty and simplicity of the song sets the tone for a play based upon fantasy, maturation and love. It is really simple special and beautiful.

~

The Music Man (Rock Island)

When did a song ever open a musical without music?

The idea of people on a train talking to the speed of the imagined train and making the train noises as it would have made them was a new approach. Stephen Sondheim recently even mentioned in a NY Times article about "Hamilton" that the opening song of"The Music Man" was pure genius. It is! You get a sense of time and place in a spoken to a rhythm cadence that is music.

You hear the idea of the entire story ahead, the perils of the traveling sales man all at once and you learn the culture of small town turn of the 20th century America all without music. The scammers that are giving the honest guys all of the trouble become evident.

It had never been done before and never since. The idea of

music being created in a song without real music was a daring and stirring all at the same time—less environment with voices creating the music is truly unique and style building for the entire musical.

30 Enjoyable Musicals That Have Faded Away

- ☆ *Of Thee I Sing*
- ☆ *The Boys From Syracuse*
- ☆ *Babes In Arms*
- ☆ *Finian's Rainbow*
- ☆ *Pal Joey*
- ☆ *Brigadoon*
- ☆ *Call Me Madam*
- ☆ *Wonderful Town*
- ☆ *The Most Happy fella*
- ☆ *Little Me!*
- ☆ *Do Re Me*
- ☆ *Fiorello*
- ☆ *Bells Are Ringing*
- ☆ *She Loves Me*
- ☆ *Carnival*
- ☆ *Man of La Mancha*
- ☆ *Zorba*
- ☆ *Applause*
- ☆ *Allegro*
- ☆ *Can Can*
- ☆ *Mame*
- ☆ *Promises, Promises*
- ☆ *Two Gentlemen of Verona*
- ☆ *Raisin*
- ☆ *Woman of the Year*
- ☆ *Mack and Mable*
- ☆ *I Do I Do!*
- ☆ *Parade*
- ☆ *On the Twentieth Century*
- ☆ *A Day In Hollywood / A Night In the Ukraine*

Of Thee I Sing

When the Gershwin's and Kaufman and Risynd wrote this Pulitzer Prize winning musical (a first musical ever to win the prize) people loved it for its satirical charm, its impression of our government and above all the wit and lunacy of our democratic system. The Gershwin music is certainly top caliber yet over time, it has become almost rarely done and it is certainly still clever, truly current with our governmental thinking and above all still truly funny.

This became the third longest running musical of the 1930 decade and although the musical won the Pulitzer Prize, George Gershwin did not as music was not at the time considered a dramatic component.

"Of Thee I Sing" needs a great revival, especially in an election year. It is too good to go away and be forgotten.

The plot has been discussed earlier.It should be seen far more often as it is clever, witty, sophisticated and stylish.

~

The Boys from Syracuse

It was a first! Shakespeare as a plot of a musical was different. Based upon "The Comedy of Errors", and the story of confused twins, the story was not new but the music was wonderful. Two wonderful Rodgers and Hart standards "This Can't be Love" and "Falling in Love with Love" come from the production.

This too is not something that we should see again as after all we do see the original it is based upon with regularity and it is hundreds of years older. One could say that Rodgers and Hart musicals are unique to them and are of a period, yet this one particularly (as well as "Babes in Arms") are somewhat quintessential of the time and deserve to be seen.

This was a groundbreaking musical approach and should be staged for today!

~

Babes In Arms

Ok so it's a little corny, and Mickey Rooney and Judy Garland probably have made it more trite and sillier than it might have been then but when you look at the score alone with the great hits"I wish I were in Love Again", "Johnny One Note", "The Lady is a Tramp", "My Funny Valentine", "Where or When" certainly don't make an evening of unheard music. It would be great to see this again, revel in the delights that we would hear and enjoy the silliness of the plot recalling the era that it came from. I vote for this one too!

Pal Joey

It was too advanced for its time and certainly was considered tasteless, odious and risqué, but it was so ground breaking, the idea of a lead that had no scruples and was amoral certainly was odd stuff for musical in 1940. Even though it was based upon the stories of John O'Hara which is a certain pedigree, the idea of a lead character of 26 being "kept" by a woman of "40" was fairly startling.

Here again musical gems are everywhere and to never see this ground breaking piece (controversial as it was in its' time) seems a real disappointment. Personally I could imagine Jeremy Jordan or Darrin Criss playing Joey opposite Idina Menzel or Sutton Foster.

The show is too interesting too be forgotten and to be remembered as the movie with Kim Novak, Rita Haworth and Frank Sinatra is really sad. It wasn't close to the original and songs got added and cut all over the place.

Finian's Rainbow

This fantasy came ahead of "South Pacific" dealing with racism, and had a great score to boot, yet it became problematic as it called for black face portrayal and that just went out of fashion. However the music of Harburg and Lane still today is wonderful. The witty satire attached to the plot about a made up state "Missitucky". The gist is that wishes and riches are not made of gold and people need to trust in one another.

The movie made in 1968 is not a great way to recall this musical, and the revival a few years back sadly did not get the run it deserved, but this is still good theatre and if handled cleverly and correctly can and should be done more often.

~

Brigadoon

Having seen this only once (and not the movie with Gene Kelly), it may be ripe for revival as well... I think it's too good to never see it, maybe it is a bit dated, and a bit frankly I'm not sure. This was the first musical by Lerner and Loewe and for that alone why shouldn't we see it? They are considered the first heirs to the Rodgers and Hammerstein model.

Yes it is fantasy about two American tourists who stumble upon a town that comes alive once every hundred years. It was made believable because of the score and the choreography of Agnes DeMille. Why wouldn't this be worth seeing again as well? "Almost Like being in Love" comes from this and not to mention "The Heather On the Hill". The whole is just too good to be lost and not seen for a hundred years as the town of the story.

Call Me Madam

Ok, let's agree this is dated in its time, 1950, but that is what makes it what it is. Political satire had been tried many times since "Of Thee I Sing", by Berlin, and by Rodgers and Hart. None of it done with great success, but this story about a socialite who gets appointed as an ambassador to a fictitious European country is really funny even if the love story part of it is a bit trite.

Yet the humor that that Lindsay and Crouse created (Mermanesque as it was) and certainly dated to its' time is a bit cutting edge in the very idea that seemed so funny then—a woman ambassador.

When Merman was given the role and the notion that a musical was being created for her based upon the real life Pearl Mesta, a socialite of the time who became an ambassador she had never even heard of Pearl Mesta. This was national news and the great leading lady had never heard of her, in itself could make a great re-write of the piece.

If you watch the movie it is really a very close reproduction of the live version (Merman and all) but if you can understand the time it is in, then you can really enjoy this. It also demonstrates why Merman never made more movies. She was just way too big for the camera in front of her.

The score is really wonderful, and Berlin never had as big a hit again so for that alone it is sheer fun. This one needs a revival (even as an antique).

~

Wonderful Town

This was revived in a staged concert style version with Donna Murphy and it was really terrific, and then moved to a real Broadway run.

It's so rarely seen and the Bernstein score so terrific it makes one wonder why. It is charming, funny, satirical, and above all if one wanted to you could almost call this #2 of the Bernstein New York trilogy. As in "On The Town" he created this imaginary wonderful vision of New York City in the 1930's.

The music is exciting, you hear the Latin rhythms he was playing with and there are the themes of music that ended up later on in "Candide". The star turn of Roz Russell is long past, but this is a great piece that should be seen. It is just another of the great musicals of the 1950's that needs to be visited.

The lament "100 ways to lose a Man" is a gem as is so much of everything else that goes on. This is a good one!

Knowing the history of the piece adds to the fun, and the look at an innocent version of New York in the 1930's adds to the mix.

~

The Most Happy Fella

This was really ambitious and so complex musically that it too is never done. In all of its years it has only been done on Broadway once since the 1956 original and it is truly operatic in form. The Loesser score with great melody and arias, was trend setting in style as well.

The music featuring several standards is wonderful and may have inspired several musicals that have come since in style and format. The story may seem a little of its time, and but seeing a masterpiece that was overshadowed by "My Fair Lady" and has faded away is really sad. This is too musically wonderful to be left in the ashes.

If you were an avid "I Love Lucy " fan you were first

exposed to this musical in an episode where the Ricardo's and the Mertz's go the theatre. The music plays while comic antics between the couples play out on screen. This script was written to assist the run of the musical in its early run. Granted, this is an opera ahead of its time of the sung through musicals of the 1970's and 1980's and is no worse for the wear.

This style is really current so we need to see this one too. One funny aside, while on a recent cruise the dancers of the ship were playing as a team in a Broadway Musical trivia, being played as a question was 'Standing on the Corner". The dancers did not know it at all but the passengers were all singing it. A new generation needs to see this one too!

~

Little Me!

Neil Simon's best work was not in any of the musicals he wrote. He didn't do the song lyrics. As a result the dialogue and the lyrics just don t match the tone of the book, but the comic drive of this musical based upon the novel by Patrick Dennis can work with a great comic talent. Cy Coleman and Carolyn Leigh wrote the words and music and several songs made hit status at the time in the early 1960's.

It was written for Sid Caesar, who had worked with Neil Simon so the script was obviously written with a good connection between the actor cast and the writer.

Having seen Martin Short one could truly see Jason Alexander, Matthew Broderick, Jim Parsons or Nathan Lane doing it as well. The conceit is one actor plays 8 husbands of the female lead. It is a slapstick skit oriented book, the score is a good one and the musical could be a real gem of an entertainment.

This too is a shame it's not seen more often

Do Re Me

This cynical musical about the recording industry and the off center people that might have inhabited it was perhaps too cynical for its time but it is still an interesting look at what it takes to succeed in a challenging irregular business world. The music is dramatic, comic, satirical and biting, with a book to match.

In the original it was Phil Silvers and Nancy Walker, it was briefly staged by the City Center Encores with Nathan Lane. It needs a well presented well done fully fledged revival.

Cynical musicals aren't so unusual today and this one about the music industry "in days of yore" would be fun to see! It has a great score as well.

Fiorello

It won a Pulitzer Prize and has had limited concert revivals. It never has had a major Broadway revival.

The story (albeit somewhat fictionalized) of the mayor of New York has a great score, wonderful satirical story telling of how politics work (the song "Politics and Poker, and "Little Tin Box") are so witty and ahead of their times that these two musical moments make it worth watching.

This was the first major success for Bock and Harnick also was in on the trend of musicals about real people that emerged at the time.

Bells Are Ringing

Well it was farfetched even in the 1950's yet the silly premise is great sitcom (of the "I love Lucy" variety). And the comic view of 1950 Manhattan a half century ago is quaint and even when it was new it was considered silly even then.

Yet the great Jule Styne score certainly gives it a wonderful evening of music and yes the story is inane but for a wonderful comic stage actress this could be a great fun piece to once again enjoy. Two great songs "The Party's over" and "Just In Time" are milestones of the score.

It is sad that the concept is so foreign in todays' world (an answering service) that the story is even lamer but for someone with wonderful comic timing and character actress ability this would be wonderful anyway! The music is modern and inventive and has so many "cityisms" not unlike "On The Town" it could almost be part of a suite of musicals about New York!

It has always been fun to watch and sad to see it fade away just because it is silly. The score is way too good for that.

~

She Loves Me

As this is being written the news is this is going to get a major revival on Broadway.

Being the first musical that Hal Prince directed and a small chamber piece with a great Bock and Harnick score, it was well received in its time, yet was not the typical musical of the era, as it was a small cast, had an operetta like feel to it and was competing against major blockbusters at the time.

Small musicals now are not so foreign and not having a dancing singing chorus is certainly nothing unusual in today's era. In its' day this was considered so very unusual that it was almost overlooked as the wonderful gem that it is.

This truly is a special piece of musical theater and hearing that it is scheduled for a major Broadway revival is really thrilling. It is a wonderful character driven musical.

~

Carnival

Not having seen this since 1965 is fairly amazing! It was considered very unique and exciting at the time with the circus theme and acts. Yet no one sees it anymore and which is a wonder! Truly intis not clear why that is the case. It was a huge hit in the 1960's. It had a great hit song "Love Makes the World Go Round". Of course the battles between David Merrick and Anna Maria Alberghetti are legendary and well renowned even to this day.

It was considered revolutionary in its day with staging that entered from the audience and circus acts that seemed to appear from everywhere. It seemed to be a great hit at the time so why haven't we seen it since. Truthfully as a kid, it seemed a bit boring but that was from a kid's perspective.

~

Man of La Mancha

One may be a bit indifferent about this one, or over the top about it. Truly this is a matter of perspective as it certainly is of its time. Some view this as a troubled cliché piece of the era, other still view it as a musical that soars. It is open for debate!

The violence of the 1960's and the turbulence felt soothed

by the ideals of Cervantes as presented here the setting for the musical during the Spanish inquisition takes place during great social upheaval. One might say we that during the 1960's we were as having as much social upheaval as the upheaval there was in the Inquisition.. Yet, there is a certain heavy handedness that the "Man of La Mancha" has to its core and it is hard to say is it dated because of the 1960's and the end of idealism that had preceded the era or is it just that it is a bit pompous?

Critics debate this one frankly. Culturally we even became tired of hearing "The Impossible Dream" as it became a cliché of itself. It sent an uplifting powerful message in the time, but now is it too innocent an idea?

Having seen the Raul Julia and the Brian Stokes Mitchell revivals one could wonder if we are ready for another one. They were truly entertaining and it showed how a classic can be interpreted into a musical that can be accessible as well as fresh. Yet it is locked into what it is! It may not even be as transporting now as it was then.

It is a piece that does command a presence; you cry at the right places, you laugh at the right places, all of which seem somehow very mechanical. Yet it has a cherished score of anthems and comic numbers that still generate great reactions.

If we are voting let's take a look again and see how it relates to now and our times of violence and radicalism. We may not be too far removed after all

~

Zorba

Having never seen this one it is just a legend! Yet a Kander and Ebb Musical based upon the movie "Zorba the Greek" can't be all bad.

True in its day it was almost the Greek answer to "Fiddler on the Roof" about an aging bigger than life hero surrounded by a cadre of ethnic characters, yet the characters have a strength that is wonderful to share. Many thought it a depressing story with little to be charmed by at the time.

It was a grittier story and did not have the universal warmth that was in "Fiddler on the Roof" (not to mention that the leads actors at the time were Fiddler Vets—Herschel Bernardi and Maria Karnilova). Yet when similarities occur to attract an audience it can detract from the piece.

The dark story still has at its core a character that is full of life against adversity and these are the ways so many musicals prosper. How does the character overcome such adversity?

It too needs a new fresh look. It has been revived about thirty years ago with success and had a Broadway run that surpassed the original. Today might be the time for a new Zorba.

(As a note of history this was the first musical to charge $15.00 for a Saturday might orchestra seat—an outrageous sum at the time! Gladly many of would pay $15.00 again vs. the huge amount of 174.00 we pay today!)

~

Applause

Oh, the magic of star appeal and the famous movie it was based upon.

This is one that might be best to let it sleep. The sensation of it was that Lauren Bacall was going to be in a musical based upon one of the great fictional movie women actresses of all times Margo Channing and "All About Eve". She in fact embodied to the nth degree the aura of the made up super star she was portraying.

Of course, Ms. Bacall had questionable talent as a musical star, although she had done a great job on Broadway in "Cactus Flower" several years prior. So why not! She had glamor, she was of a certain age, and she had the gutsy style that the character required without even uttering a word. She had presence and that famous throaty laugh. She was already a legend.

The challenge in the book was that nothing from the movie could be used as the rights to the film were off limits, but the book it had been based upon was available. So the story and the characters could be used but the great movie basis could not. That then created a reinvention of what was so familiar.

If you are really curious go and watch some You Tube clips and see for yourself that it is a curiosity at best in todays' era and although it was a huge success at the time based upon the star appeal it just is not current enough in today's world to spend time with. Lauren Bacall does not come across well in the taped versions you can see on YOUTUBE. That great charisma isn't totally lost, yet one wonders what was she really doing there?

Fabulous as she was at the time and certainly career building for her, she looks out of place. She won praise for her gutsy portrayal and the chance she took, but as we look back was it the act she could get away with it or was she really that wonderful?

Sometimes it is best to remember the past and forget the reality of it. This musical even in its recording makes one wonder.

It might be fun to put Patti Lupone or Idina Menzel in it and take a look, but frankly they miss the basic over the hill star power that makes the role work. Yet they need the legend that Lauren Bacall had to make the work really shine and there are not too many of those left anymore.

~

Allegro

Having seen a revival of this one, and liking it the idea that there is Rodgers and Hammerstein that is not so familiar is pretty terrific.

It was way ahead of its time with a plot that was about an "everyman" with a time span to match. It was traditional in scope and contemporary in structure. This startled the audiences in 1947 and the over choreographed support behind the actors didn't help. The dance sequences limited the original appeal and the audiences did not know what to make of it.

Yet the story is a good one, and the music is wonderful!

We have matured a great deal in 70 years and this musical has a very interesting ability to be presented with gusto, passion and dignity. Imagine a rarely seen Rodgers and Hammerstein, isn't that reason enough? It is too good a piece even if flawed to be totally ignored and the style they were reaching for certainly is evident.

The piece as a nonspecific time line (era) story had the style of a contemporary musical and felt very fresh in its story telling. Perhaps it seems too remote in the past of an archive to achieve a success but knowing how Lincoln Center has re-created their great works maybe it is time for this one.

Can Can

Well the book is a bit silly and trite. However to hear "I love Paris" and where it came from is not all bad.

True, the idea of indecency in Paris in the 1890's and a judge who falls in love with the woman who owns the venue where the indecent dance is performed seems oddly placed—but so what! The book may not be the most outstanding but a classic is a classic. The music is Great Cole Porter and has standards that people love to hear.

There has been talk of re-writing the book to have it make more sense from a logical point of view and that would be a great idea, but in the meantime the score is so good so what of the plot is a little ridiculous.

It has great dance sequences and in the early 1950's proved that Cole Porter music could catch the ear of the listening public. I'd buy seats to see it.

~

Mame

To be honest I did see a fairly flat revival of this one With Christine Baranski directed by Eric Schaeffer at the Kennedy Center a few years back and I wanted really love it as it is a favorite of mine. It is such a great story about a madcap lady and the nephew she raises. There is nothing shocking or satirical about it any longer but yet it is a heartwarming and wonderful story.

With one or two exceptions it has a great score (you have to forgive Jerry Herman I guess for copying his own music out of "Hello Dolly!), yet the story is pretty wonderful and it is a great show case for a comic actress who can sing and another comic dead pan actress who can be her sidekick.

It may be a vehicle of its time; the story is still a good one. After all it is what it is, but you do have to love it. It made a musical theatre star out of Angela Lansbury who was in a career dead-end and it could do it again for the right person. It might be fun to have a contest among ourselves as to who might we cast to play Auntie Mame?

~

Promises, Promises!

Having seen the recent revival with Sean Hayes and Kristin Chenowith who were both wrong for it one can only seem to wonder if this is was even truly revivable or just trying to capitalize on the "Mad Men" craze at the time.

Sean Hayes was mechanical and technically correct but it was hard to buy him as the sad sack cynical guy trying to get ahead. His singing did not have a sad edge to it yet he really was doing what the music asked of him. In fact he seemed too technical and precise. As a listener one should not have to hear a singer's precision. His comic ability was fine but it was wrong.

Kristin Chenowith was just totally wrong. They had no chemistry and you not could quite see what they might see in each other. She was just too cutesy for my taste and looked like a mismatch for him.

Oh there was that great Bacharach score, but you know this is one that could have had a partially black cast or even Lea Salonga in the lead. It was way too sterile for its own good. It looked great, but the package was off.

They couldn't even tour it—if that tells you something. It was just too un-clever for its own good. It may be best to let this one just sit and be a relic where the pop standards are the memory.

Part of the challenge is the Neil Simon book which lacks the satirical edge of the movie it was taken from. He matched the tone of the score but the score maybe was too "pop" for the tone of what the story is about.

~

Two Gentlemen of Verona

Oh the era that created the rock musical! See what "Hair" did for us. We had to have imitators and there were many of them and most of the really not worth seeing today. In its day this was a very dynamic telling of Shakespeare. History does odd things, the year this musical debuted it was up against 'Follies" and who would imagine in retrospect that "Follies" did not win the Best Musical Tony and this did!

It is also hard to imagine that the times of the original so desperately seeking the young "hippie" crowd responded to this as well as it did!

Having seen it in its premiere run—it was truly enjoyable and seemingly was really terrific and a lot of fun. It had a wild pop rock score and the Shakespeare set to music was really terrific. It even had Raul Julia in his break out performance. Time has just not been good to the musical translation at all. It has all of the good sound of a 70's rock score but it just gets very tired the more you hear it.

It was also color blind casting at the time which was radical and very exciting, actually groundbreaking with its very integrated cast.

It was revived by "Shakespeare in the Park" a few season back and it was greatly anticipated and did not generate enough buzz to move it to a Broadway house then. That said it is even too harsh for high schools and has not been on that circuit either.

This is a milestone that is best left alone. It is sad to say that a once clever translation of Shakespeare just isn't good enough for now.

(As an aside there is a rock musical of "Twelfth Night" called "Your Own Thing" also from the same era that has not aged well at all on any level.)

~

Raisin

Arena Stage in DC was very bold and worked with the Lorraine Hansbury play "Raisin in the Sun" and made it into a musical. As Sondheim says some characters just don't sing and this is one of those translations that over time is evident. It was also the time of "black" musicals and the idea of turning this well regarded play into a musical seemed like it could cross over the color barrier. The story of a black family trying to buy a home in a white suburb and the specific complications of racism and values in an "upwardly mobile" black vs. white society in the 1950's was the theme.

At the time it certainly had a mildly successful run and did please many people as the book was based upon something strong, but it hasn't aged well either and although the original morphed into a play about what happened years after the end of "Raisin in the Sun" (Clyborne Park) it did a better job than the musicalization of the original story. The musical just tried to be a book piece with music and the work just did not mesh.

Black musicals were a fashion, as this era also produced "The Wiz", and "Purlie" neither of which is truly worth seeing today. They just have not aged well.

It might be interesting to see if this really is revivable but there is not real hope for it.

The Wiz

Well take a tale everyone knows and turn it on its side a bit and make it a black musical you can create a mega hit. It ran for over four years in the 1970's and it was clever and had a rock score that seemed to make the musical relevant. These things just don't age well.

Opening night in New York they posted a closing notice but somehow a miracle happened it ran.

In retrospect it ran way too long, and when you look at it today you have to really scratch your head. It was sort of clever but not really, it was sort of fun, for a while, and the overblown vision of the tale it copied was hard to digest if you had too much to eat before the show.

This is one of those musicals that in its over amped state just starts to sound monotonous and tires the audience out way before the final curtain. Yes it is a great idea, and frankly was clever in a tiresome way, in retrospect it too is best left alone.

It was a skit, almost as if the Carol Burnett show had done it. The story was too laden with messages of the day and seemed to be trying too hard to prove its point.

~

Woman of the Year

Star vehicles often seem great in their time and in hindsight that is all they were.

With the success that Lauren Bacall created in "Applause" it seemed a terrific idea to say that it would be a slam dunk to create another vehicle for her with a classic movie as the basis of the musical. Hence the first movie of the Tracy-Hepburn relationship seemed like a great musical vehicle. Well at least on paper!

Quoting Mr. Sondheim once again, sometimes characters just don't sing, well beside the obvious that Ms. Bacall didn't, her stage presence alone made it happen. She had her classy sophistication that truly was mesmerizing across the footlights and once again she proved that her star power was radioactive.

The musical packed them in primarily due to the star, and the Kander and Ebb score certainly was not their finest, but there sure isn't much there to get excited about in terms of story and character singing.

In reality take away the glitter of Ms. Bacall and what you have left is sort of a dud. She toured in it so all of those across America could worship her as they did, but still when you left the theatre it was the memory of the glittering Hollywood legend that you were left with.

~

Mack and Mable

Jerry Herman wrote musicals with female star characters in the limelight, Dolly, and Mame as his most famous. Yet this idea of writing a musical about the antics of the Mack Sennet movies and legend of his love affair with Mabel Normand seemed to have a great potential. Michael Stewart and Gower Champion were aboard with the project. It was the "Hello Dolly" team, all over again.

Jerry Herman wrote his best score ever, beautiful ballads, rollicking movie making musical numbers and had two perfect stars in Robert Preston and Bernadette Peters in her break out lead performance.

Yet the book was awkward and confusing, not well handled and the era of the traditional book musical was going through its own audience challenges for acceptance. Was it the era or the piece. Those involved did not view it objectively at the time as the self-congratulating on their accomplishments ruined objectivity and the book dragged down the musical badly as there were no likable qualities in anyone present.

This was of course the early Sondheim era, and the rock musical era to boot, so adding it all up it did not make" Mack and Mabel" easy, especially with characters that were so unlikable that you wondered why anyone would bother.

It was revived in London several years ago and there were improvements to the book. Yet still it has languished over the years and has become well-loved because of the truly wonderful score. This proved to be a devastating failure to all involved.

After the failure of this it took Jerry Herman 14 years to create another new work and his last sadly, as he felt he would never write another musical again as he had nothing more to prove.

Sadly, "Mack and Mabel" deserves some sort of revised opportunity. There is some great music at its core and there could be a reward here to resurrect it.

I Do I Do!

A simple two character history of a marriage that has good heat, honest emotion, and little expense should make money for anyone that produces it.

Go back to the 1960's and it had Robert Preston and Mary Martin not to mention many other star powered teams such as Carol Burnett and Rock Hudson. It always made money for whoever produced it.

There are surely teams of people that would make it pop now. Imagine Hugh Jackman for one or Matthew Broderick and Sara Jessica! Talk about a powerhouse and a brief run it would rake it in. It is a simple piece not overly complicated and it is very lovely!

~

Parade

It's not a light entertainment that is for sure, but the story of a man who is wrongfully accused of a rape in the south in the pre-World War I era, with Anti-Semitism as its sub-text is a powerful musical.

Being wrongly accused, because you did not fit into the mainstream culture still does resonate today. This and anti-Semitism are the core of the horrific story. It does not make for a pleasant, light evening, but it was well revived in its' time and in revivals has done well. The musical has gone on to be very well appreciated.

Hal Prince directed and with the music of Jason Robert Brown it packs a serious punch. The poignancy of the couple, who fall in love in the midst of adversity, is the core of the work. It makes the tragic outcome—the miscarriage of justice—even more disturbing

It is an important piece, Alfred Uhry writing a tale of events in his native Atlanta reminds us that the world should never be proud of these events. Uhry had a personal connection of sorts to the story. Yet the subject matter is tough going and requires an audience to hunker down for the sad ending to come.

The music is majestic and with great passion, the writing eloquent and poignant. This is too important a piece, to be forgotten and never seen, difficult a piece as it is.

~

1600 Pennsylvania Avenue

This was a piece commissioned for the Bi-centennial from Leonard Bernstein. During tryouts based upon critical and audience reception to Bernstein's new creation he was so disheartened by it that he wouldn't even allow a recording. The music was edited without his permission creating inexcusable treatment to the composer.

Essentially it was the story of the early presidents in the White House (hence the title) with the history that those times recalled. You do hear, once in a while, music sung from this and of course it is Bernstein music which is always wonderful. Theatre historians consider this a well forgotten masterpiece and the fact the Alan J. Lerner's book was not well executed did not help. The musical version of the Bernstein score has been done as a cantata with classical not Broadway singers with positive response.

This may need the re-examination that "Candide" received in the 1970's; a more creative and revolutionary approach to what might be an incredible event. This could really be a "wow"

~

On the Twentieth Century

Recently this rarely done musical "operetta" style piece was revived on Broadway with Kristin Chenoweth and Peter Gallagher to great reviews and was first time since its original production in 1978 that it had been revived. In its original it featured Madelyn Kahn as Lily Garland the former girlfriend/protégé actress of Oscar Jaffee the former high priest of Broadway who is now down on his luck.

One has to look at the timing of when pieces arrive! Looking back at them, sometimes can give a new awakening. This was "The Chorus Line" era and the non-linear concept musical was the ruling style. Traditional book musicals were having a difficult time getting traction and attention.

It was hard enough for the now recognized masterpieces to compete in the era (Chicago did not achieve great fame as we have discussed for 20 years). This truly atmospheric witty beautifully sung piece got lost in the shuffle as well.

It had Cy Coleman Music with Comden and Greene Lyrics, it was directed by Hal Prince and did run for almost a year, but it should have had a far greater success as it was based upon a well know classic movie and nostalgia was a very prominent craze in the time period.

Yet, it literally faded away and just sat around as a distantly recalled relic of musicals past. Sadly the recent Roundabout theatre revival just did not plan a long enough run and it ran from February 2015-July 2015 and so if it could only tour the greater world would get to know it.

A Day In Hollywood / A Night In the Ukraine

Thinking back having seen this three times in the 1970's when it was new, it was great fun! It was a two act "review" where the first act was a beautifully sung and choreographed tribute to old Hollywood with a cast of 6. The satire of Hollywood was glorious.

The first act, *A Day in Hollywood*, a send up of classic Hollywood songs of the 1930s performed by singers and dancers representing ushers from Graumann's Chinese Theatre, and features a significant amount well imagined tap sequences. The second act, *A Night in the Ukraine*, is loosely based on Chekov's one-act play "The Bear" and is presented in the style of a Marx Brothers movie; the cast then assumes the roles in character of the Marx Brothers.

In a review of a regional production the reviewer from "The New York Times" commented that the musical "...has a hybrid score that lists music by Frank Lazarus, with book and lyrics by Dick Vosburgh, additional songs composed by Jerry Herman and a solid midsection medley devoted to the prolific composer of popular movie music, Richard Whiting. We are treated to a pleasant musical grab bag"

It is really fun, and it has to be cast with a cast that can emulate the zany brothers fairly well, but that aside it needs to be seen again as it is a wonderful fun theatrical event.

23 Flops That (Based on Pedigree) Should Have Been Hits

- ☆ *On a Clear Day*
- ☆ *Do I hear a waltz*
- ☆ *High Spirits*
- ☆ *Pickwick*
- ☆ *Camelot*
- ☆ *Mack and Mable*
- ☆ *Boy From OZ*
- ☆ *Assassins*
- ☆ *Merrily We Roll Along*
- ☆ *Passion*
- ☆ *Allegro*
- ☆ *Dear World*
- ☆ *Do Re Me*
- ☆ *Little Me*
- ☆ *110 in the Shade*
- ☆ *Hallelujah Baby*
- ☆ *She Loves Me*
- ☆ *Chess*
- ☆ *Aspects of love*
- ☆ *Sunset Boulevard*
- ☆ *Victor Victoria*
- ☆ *Ragtime*
- ☆ *Tarzan*

On a Clear Day You Can See Forever

Ok let's all agree this is a story that is a bit far-fetched and the awful revival a few years back with Harry Connick JR. was truly laughable and inane, yet the basic premise was interesting and the small cast could make it a profitable venture.

It had a lot going for it at the time when it was new!

Alan Jay Lerner was always fascinated with the idea of ESP and partnered with Burton Lane (who wrote a great score that to this day has produced some great standards).

The plot was basically a young woman goes to a psychiatrist to stop smoking gets hypnotized and then it seems she has lived another life in the past. It is an intriguing idea and new for the time it was a small cast without big chorus numbers and truly more like a play with music. It was a very intimate piece and should have worked. Truthfully the story is one you have to buy into and you either did or you didn't and there was nothing truly logical about it. Yet if you saw good people in it, the story was not totally off putting and was a pleasant diversion. Truly who can be sure if it was worth re-doing and the Streisand movie didn't help it any either.

To enjoy this go buy and original cast recording and listen.

~

Do I Hear a Waltz?

When Oscar Hammerstein was dying he told Stephen Sondheim that one day there would come a time when Richard Rodgers would come to him with the request to write a musical. The play "Time Of the Cuckoo" ended up being the project. The result is Rodgers and Sondheim worked together. To hear Sondheim on the subject he does not recall this very pleasantly as Rodgers was of another era, and not in sync with the Sondheim vision for a musical. Also it has been said that Rodgers treated Sondheim horribly and the two hardly had a pleasant relationship.

It was not a great partnership and the story based upon the "Time of The Cuckoo" and then the movie "Summertime"

(With Katherine Hepburn) was a somewhat sad tale of a spinster schoolteacher who would know when she fell in love.

Sondheim believed that the spinster character on a summer trip to Italy, didn't have a real song to sing (not that there weren't some written but that the character just didn't sing) Sondheim also felt that at the end a great song should be written for her to sing and then the character would in some way come alive musically as well.

Rodgers couldn't quite get that and thus the idea of a dance less musical was created. It needed something so the Song" Do I Hear A Waltz" was written with Herbert Ross adding the choreography. Sondheim and Rodgers were on a creative crash course. Sondheim was full of a creative new vision and of course Richard Rodgers was at the end of his.

Arthur Laurent's wrote the book and the original vision was for Mary Martin to play the lead. She then was viewed as too old and the casting shifted. Rodgers by this time had a severe drinking problem and the project was plagued with challenges because of that.

On the one hand you would think (wow!) a Richard Rodgers/Sondheim Musical should really work well! To his credit, Sondheim stuck with it due to his regard for what Hammerstein had given him, but Rodgers was a miserable character at this point and everyone was at war including the director who cast Elizabeth Allen in the part and she was perceived too cold and lifeless. This became a project run through indifference.

Taubman of the New York Times Said, "The authors . . . have accomplished their conversion from the play with tact and grace. They have not attempted a complete transformation. On the other hand, they have not cheapened or falsified the play . . . They were wise not to overload the musical with production numbers; their taste was unexceptionable when they chose not to turn their work into a brash, noisy affair, which would have been out of keeping with their theme. At the same time one cannot suppress a regret that they failed to be bolder. For there are times, particularly in the early stages, when the songs are merely a decoration. They give the impression that they are there because a musical requires music. They do not translate the story into the fresh and marvelous language that the rich resources of the musical stage make possible."

Over time Sondheim saw potential in the piece but felt the Rodgers music was a really not an asset. It has since been reworked but still one must wonder is it worth the bother.

~

High Spirits

Noel Coward and Musicals just don't seem to work! There never was a successful one. You take the witty dialogue and the British manners that his comedies utilized and then add music it is not a solid mixture. British manners don't get sung well!

Beatrice Lillie starred in the expanded role of the medium Madam Arcati and the book closely followed the Coward dialogue and plot, but it never really took off. Adding music created an added muddle to the satire of the plot. Coward also hated Lillie. Coward had dreamed it would be Gwen Verdon which would have even created a different musical than the one that was created, it certainly would have had lots of dance sequences but this was an imagined hit and never really made it.

~

Pickwick

After the success of "Oliver!" other Dickens novels seemed ripe for musical adaptation. Leslie Bricusse wrote the score and the sets and entire staging seemed to be copied directly from the vision of "Oliver!" It did have one great song, "If I Ruled the World" but the magic of "Oliver" just did not carry over even if David Merrick was the producer and should have made it more of a success.

Charlotte Rae who went on to bigger fame later in TV was in this production and BBC even did a filmed version, but it just did not connect. Sometimes you can think you have all of the pieces in place and they just do not fit.

Copying a success does not mean that the copy will be as good as the first. A formula does not always supply what you need.

~

Camelot

Probably one of the most famous misguided musicals ever is "Camelot." Lerner and Loewe being fresh from "My Fair Lady" and "GIGI" success felt the idea of writing a musical about the Arthurian legend seemed a great idea. The truth is many people do not realize that Camelot was not a success. It basks in a glow that has nothing to do with the reality of the musical.

The entire "My Fair Lady" team was re-engaged starting with Moss Hart, Lerner and Loewe.

The book the <u>Once and Future King</u> was the source material. Lerner said that if this was not a success this would be his last musical. He was going through a divorce and his mind was not into the project. The strong cast that included

Richard Burton, Julie Andrews, Roddy McDowell and a new discovery Robert Goulet enhanced the project immensely.

The original production clocked in at 4.5 hours and needed drastic editing and reworking. In the midst of this Moss Hart had a heart attack and the direction was taken, lamely, over by Lerner. It did not get all that much shorter. The two hour and 40 minute optimal running time was still elusive.

Just days before the official opening Moss Hart was released from the hospital and more cuts and additions were made.

The reviews were mixed and if you needed to sell tickets to a Broadway show in this era you called upon dear Ed Sullivan who could work wonders in many cases. In the case of "Camelot" it worked. Ed Sullivan approached Lerner and Loewe to create a special segment on his show to celebrate the fifth anniversary of "My Fair Lady". Instead they decided that they would not use the previous hit but would instead use four highlights from Camelot! This helped sell a tremendous amount of tickets and a new heartthrob was born to the show stopper "If Ever I Would Leave You". Any success"Camelot" developed had to be because of this. The audience associated this as the new "My Fair Lady" and it certainly was not, but the score still sounded great and television was a great validator in that era.

The book was a mess as it had characters come and go (Pellinore and Morgan le Fay) with very little to do. Each was disconnected from the real plot. There were musical numbers that seemed to come from nowhere and the whole idea of Julie Andrews bringing down a kingdom over her beguiling combustible sexuality and starting a war was never really believable. Truthfully, that wasn't exactly well developed in the story either and was mildly presented as a plot device. The performers were all top notch but their strong stage charisma was not going to solve the problem.

The show ran two years and was connected ultimately with the Kennedy Administration. JFK was a class mate of Allan Jay Lerner at Harvard. He liked the album and it had been mentioned how much he loved the music form the cast album and listened to it. After the assassination Jackie Kennedy gave two interviews. In one of the interviews she mentioned how JFK liked listening to the album. She then declared that the final lyric of "Camelot" is how she hopes memories will be for the Kennedy administration and she quoted them.

> "Don't let it be forgot
> that once there was a spot,
> for one brief, shining moment
> that was known as Camelot"

This clever bit of visualization labeled the Kennedy Administration "Camelot" from that point forward. This then gave the musical a pedigree it truly did not deserve. It was never really the success it might have been and if you see it today you cherish it as a memory of at time not because it is a great musical.

Having seen a credible revival a few years back I thought that it was a good as it gets. It is lumbering, bloated and a bit odd how characters come and go, yet the music does save it from being a total disaster and it does have a pageantry that gives it a wonderful magic even if it is in brief snippets.

~

Mack and Mable

This too has been discussed earlier.

Jerry Herman was writing musicals but not since "Mame" had he had a musical success. He had written a musical starring Angela Lansbury based upon the" Madwoman of Chaillot" but it was not a success and the next musical choice he thought would be a great hit based upon Mack Sennett and Mabel Normand of the silent movie era.

The initial previews of the musical received fair to warm reviews out of town. but the story with two truly unredeemable dark characters in the script never really gelled. Robert Preston and Bernadette Peters had questionable chemistry on stage and although two masterful performers could not pull off what the roles in the weak script required.

Another challenge was this was a book musical in an era when the traditional book musical was falling out of favor.

Visually Gower Champion created strong images using his great choreographic style and the musical looked terrific. His brightness was in deep contrast to the overall mood of the piece which was a somber story of a tragic love affair. The music, a true favorite of the composer also was somewhat brighter than the tone of the script Michael Stewart had created and in the total assessment it just did not all fit. Audiences couldn't warm up to a down trodden story about a cocaine addicted movie star. It was almost a who cares as she wasn't interesting enough nor famous enough to a modern generation.

The show became unbalanced and over hyped. After all it was a Jerry Herman musical and the expectations were very high. Sometimes those in charge can't fall in love with their own work and have to be objective about what is on stage.

Oddly the score was not nominated for a Tony Award, sadly, as to many it is his best. To this day this is a recording that creates listening enjoyment. The music Herman composed for this piece is his most real score he ever wrote.

"Mack and Mabel" has achieved cult status and is always spoken about for a revival. Yet having been done many times outside the US it has never been done here. The Production at the Shaw festival directed by Molly Smith was widely praised and yet it too never caught on for revival .

Truly this is an example of not reading the climate when creating a new work.

~

The Boy From OZ

Juke Box musicals have become the rage and taking the musical of Peter Allen and staging his life to his music was at best moderately clever but his songs for the most part did not fit his life story and seeing caricatures of Liza Minnelli and Judy Garland on stage telling a life story that seemed one dimensional just didn't help.

Peter Allen was a larger than life guy and certainly Hugh Jackman cast as the very creative Allen helped but none of it seemed real and at best it was cartoonish.

At best the show was a Hugh Jackman tour de force. It recouped it entire investment not because it was good but probably because Hugh Jackman took his short off twice and the audience full of women went nuts. The reason you went was to see Hugh! While there you had to ignore the ridiculous event of the evening. It was tough to see cartoon style Judy Garland and Liza Minelli on stage—it was almost as if Carol Burnett did a send up from her variety show.

Yet it was a hit of sorts, Hugh won all sorts of awards and frankly elevated him to mega star with real Broadway chops. It was amazing to see him. Yet the show was itself a disaster.

At the end of his contract the producers could not find anyone to replace him. They considered and hoped for Ricky Martin, but he did not agree. The story may have hit too close to home, who knows but without Hugh there was simply no show.

~

Assassins

Some say this was a strange topic for a Musical, the people that assassinated Presidents.

Sondheim thought to get into the heads of why someone could become so disenfranchised and disconnected from society that they would go think they could take society into their own hands and shoot a president was fascinating. As odd as this is, think about the events today where a single killer takes a weapon in to their own hands and fires it in a school or a movie theatre.

As all of Sondheim's masterpieces do, this has that peculiar presence about it, asking one to think and react. It is an acquired taste, but it is still a challenging piece of musical theatre for the audience.

~

Merrily We Roll Along

A magical team that has great reviews, great vision and great appetite for doing new and different shouldn't have such a flop!

Hal Prince and Stephen Sondheim have always had great musical combustion. From 1970-1979 they created masterpiece after masterpiece and were both envied and reviled for what they could create as a team.

Hal Prince and Sondheim have both shared the story that Mrs. Prince thought it would be wonderful to see a musical with young and talented actors mounting a new work. Intrigued by the idea the duo sought to take a Kaufman and Hart play which is about two writers and runs backwards in time and create a musical from it.

This is not so simple when it comes to the creative process. The audience meets the main characters at the end of their relationship. It is not told in flashback it is told in reverse which is jarring in its very nature, Just as you get accustomed to where you are in time you are somewhere earlier, and then earlier and even earlier. It never moves back to the present for the “aha’s” of time.

As with most musicals prior to this era, they were worked on out of town and away from the nearby rumor mills and the critic’s eyes. The costs were such that taking the show out of town first was no longer feasible so it was done in NYC.

The very core of the idea that young actors would play the roles was a mistake as they did not have the maturity to carry of the earlier older scenes. It was a difficult situation. Yet the show is a far better entertainment than first imagined. It is funny, clever, musically outstanding and above all and the saddest—the end of the Sondheim / Prince collaboration.

Frank Rich wrote “As we all should probably have learned by now, to be a Stephen Sondheim fan is to have one’s heartbroken at regular intervals.”

Clive Barnes wrote, “Whatever you may have heard about it—go and see it for yourselves. It is far too good a musical to be judged by those twin kangaroo courts of word of mouth and critical consensus.”[

Over years “Merrily” has developed a real cult following and has been revived and played with significantly more interest.

There are several recordings that demonstrate there was more here than the critics initially saw. It is a truly terrific evening of musical theater.

~

Passion

Romantic, lush, beautiful, melodic, elegant are all adjectives that can describe this amazingly exquisite work. Yet Sondheim is never easy accessible theatre.

This sweeping odd romance is based upon an Italian movie "Passione D'amore" a story of a very handsome soldier who is deeply in love with a beautiful woman. However he is chased with deep passion by a horribly ugly woman and he repels her on sight. The story is how true love can grow besides deep passions that interfere and develop our loves. It is a complicated retelling of the classic line "Beauty is only skin deep"

It won the Tony for Best Musical, Best Score, and then failed to run. It is too powerfully beautiful a piece to have had that treatment.

Yet it was also the 1990's and musical theater was caught in a creative dungeon. First there was the style of the overblown British import and the new rising Disney cartoon musical.

"Passion" just did not fit. It is an incredible piece so strong in its presentation the audience never claps for anything until it is over as the musical is so expressive and connected to the character it is hard to see where it begins and ends. Having seen this several times it becomes clear that the overpowering passions enrapture the audiences and they become numb.

It is not dull, never boring, but truly a beautiful emotional experience. The great news is that PBS filmed it and it can be seen on DVD. It is an exquisite piece of musical theater that is haunting and riveting. It is too good to be never seen.

Allegro

Much has been written about this great disappointment, even here, that came with the completion of the Rodgers and Hammerstein Musical. It was the next one written after "Carousel "and frankly the team was looking at innovation and again trying to re-invent the art form.

It had an "everyman" plot and Agnes DeMille had created a Greek chorus that danced in commentary on the events of the characters. Having seen this some years ago stripped down without the unneeded choreography it was truly enjoyable.

However in 1947 when this was conceived it was far too vague for the theatre goer at the time, and in fact even though it passes through many decades seemed way to offbeat and Avant-Garde.

Yet today with the approach that musicals have taken this is far more acceptable for the average person.

So to follow "Carousel" and "Oklahoma" the expectations were high. The same team had been reunited and this should have by all accounts been a huge success. It sadly was not and this bothered the team greatly as they thought they had created a great work of art. It truly was not the imagined success by any means and although Rodgers and Hammerstein had other missteps this hurt more as it was after two major successes.

The pedigree alone should have made it work, but that sometimes too doesn't mean success is at hand.

To learn firsthand about the trials and tribulations about

mounting a musical a young Stephen Sondheim was a $25 week gofer and witnessed the creative frustration as they tried to mount this unusual piece.

~

Dear World

When you think about pedigree, this production should have worked. Sometimes all involved get too carried away and disagreements amongst the creative team caused many resignations and frustrations. At the time Jerry Herman had three shows running simultaneously on Broadway and this too should have on the surface been a huge success.

Angela Lansbury starred, fresh out of her "Mame" glory and was a huge box office asset. Angela won a Tony for her portrayal of the lead character. In fact the Herman score has some fantastic music, including an exciting trio for the three women characters and has truly reached a cult status.

Closing after a very short run, Jerry Herman, Lawrence and Lee the writers all looked at what went wrong. They felt it was overweighed and should have been a chamber piece rather than a bloated Broadway Musical.

It has been reworked and frankly as a chamber piece can be mounted very well. Yet again this is one of those great opportunities that had tremendous promise and went awry because of the lack of clear focus and wisdom of how to go about the piece.

Do Re Me!

This should have worked, but then again most producers go after something they think will be a success or they wouldn't go after it at all.

A satirical musical about the recording industry with a great big television star Phil Slivers, a great s Jule Styne score and a book by Garson Kanin you would think hit in the making?

The New York Times called it "fast loud and occasionally funny". It felt incomplete to many and just never clicked. It was revived by City Center Encores and did not fare much better. It just did not work well enough.

This is just another example of a good pedigree does not necessarily make a hit show. Listen to the original or the City Center recording both are great!

~

Little Me

Patrick Dennis had already written a terrific popular novel "Auntie Mame". It would seem that a musical based upon another of his novels written with Sid Caesar starring and his favorite writer Neil Simon writing with a score written by Cy Coleman could work .There even were two hits that were picked up and played on the radio, recorded by various singers of the day.

Bob Fosse choreographed and to Neil Simon this was a major opportunity. With Sid Caesars comic reputation you would assume this would be a huge hit and be a highly successful musical. To be honest looking at the Musicals that Neil Simon crafted none are great scripts. His comic tone never seems to match the musical numbers and the transposition always seems like "now it is song time"

It is a hard piece to pull off as you need a comic talent so vast and manic that it takes enormous talent and skill. The play conceit is that one person plays eight husbands of the female character.

It was one skit after another right off of 1950's television variety show. The score is a good one yet somehow all of the zaniness goes into overdrive and it wears out the audience, too loud and faced paced. In fairness this was at the start of Sid Caesar's long decline and it may have showed. The show ran about 7 months in 1962. Truly, that was not fair to the piece.

Today with Nathan Lane for sure, or Jason Alexander it would be terrific. The Martin Short revival a few years back was really enjoyable. Maybe it needs a good solid revival but this too is an example of it should have been a real winner.

~

She Loves Me

A wonderful chamber piece that was the basis of two MGM films "The Shop around the Corner" and "The Good Old Summertime" should have been great creative energy for wonderful gem of a musical. It is small intimate, charming and delightful. It had no chorus a small cast and as George Abbott told Hal Prince the audience will not get it—where is the chorus and dancing numbers? Bock and Harnick wrote a delightful operetta like score and the plot, two lovelorn loners writing letters to each other (working side by side) hating each other in real life but loving each other in letters was the plot.

It is a delicious musical and was meant to star Julie Andrews but she was tied up making a soon to be famous movie, "Mary Poppins". Instead they cast Barbara Cook, Jack Cassidy, and Daniel Massey.

Joe Maseteroff and Bock and Harnick created a great piece together.

It just never really connected. It was too small for the time besides it opened in the spring of 1963 and by late fall with tragedy surrounding everyone after the assassination many musicals closed and this was another one.

George Abbott may have been correct. Maybe it was too small a piece for the time. It was a perfect gem, however and in revivals it has been well received and has created a cult following. It is a special piece, charming and delightful.

~

110 in the Shade

A famous Katherine Hepburn movie, of a well-known play "The Rainmaker" should have worked. This is a simple story with music by Tom Jones and Harvey Schmidt, after writing 'The Fantasticks". It should have also been a big hit.

Yet, sometimes you have to look at the competition and see what the audiences are responding to and small simple stories just were not the right thing at the time. It opened one month before the Kennedy assassination and frankly that may have put a damper on it. The story was not bright enough to capture interest after that very dark period and suddenly the major attractions of the day were "Hello Dolly" and "Funny Girl."

It is beautifully melodic and the story about a lonely dry "spinster" in a hot Midwest drought ridden town with a con man who promises to make it rain are the "stuff" of musical fantasy.

Nash who wrote the script based upon his original play

kept the tone and opened it up to get townspeople involved but it is still a small story. Small stories were not popular at the time and intimate chamber pieces which in reality this surely was (even though chorus moments were added) may have been perceived as inference to the whole script. It was ahead of its' time.

This too in another time might have worked better. There was an Audra MacDonald revival a few years back that did get glowing reviews, yet won no awards and just did not garner any attention. Some musicals are cursed that way. They could be wonderful but frankly just don't ignite the theatre going public to react.

~

Hallelujah Baby!

Almost as if it took a clue form Rodgers and Hammerstein's "Allegro", Jule Styne with Comden and Greene Lyrics, and Arthur Laurents book tried to create a story of black America in the story of an everywoman. It was certainly meant to be topical, the story allegedly universal and above all musically interesting with the casting of Leslie Uggams as the lead who continues through time as a black character in America. This too had a great pedigree going in. It was also of an era where there was a focus to create black themed productions.

The idea was originally to have Lena Horne who was herself so committed to the struggle of African American women in America, that by the time it really got the go-ahead she frankly lost interest in doing it. By compromising with Uggams the show seemed to lose its bite. Yet it won a best musical Tony in 1967. The reality was that the creative team lost interest in the project and did the best they could with what they had but it just did not have the edge they had hoped for.

However times were also changing for American musicals and the hippie culture and the events of 1969 did not help propel this musical to connect with its audiences and gain wide acceptance or interest.

Once again it's the story of pedigree and timing. The team was so experienced and the beneficiaries of some great musicals, yet the approach to the topic in the civil rights turmoil of the time just trivialized the material.

Having seen it on the 2005 Arena Stage revival the piece had little to offer frankly that was exciting or groundbreaking and although it was interesting to see as a curiosity it just was that, a curiosity.

IN 1967 it was probably also just a curiosity.

~

Chess

Concept albums being made into live Musicals seemed to have reached their peak. With smashes such as "Evita" and Les Miserables" forebears of the genre you would think "Chess" would have succeeded. "Chess" never made a dime and lost $6 million in its US production. The idea was so convoluted that even Andrew Lloyd Weber passed on it with Tim Rice. It was a political story with a chess match as the metaphor of crossed alliances.

"Chess" seemed to be an ideal fit for the tastes of the time with bigger being better and totally sung through being a style of choice. All of the components seemed to line up to make this a success.

It was a technological production and had many exciting moments but the total package was large and loud, not at all connecting with the audiences. It was in a way pretentious, pompous and overblown but inside was a simple low key story among a few people. The "little "story was overpowered by the overblown surroundings.

The irony of this was that the concept album that was used to create interest in the musical opportunity received great reviews. Once on stage it was seen as overly long. Bloated, terribly messy in it's' book, improbable and silly.

Frank Rich of the New York Times said "has the theatrical consistency of quicksand" and described it as "a suite of temper tantrums, [where] the characters yell at each other to rock music"

In fact some reviewers thought it assaulted the audience with over amped scene after scene of non-stop music.

It even was a PBS concert version with Josh Groban and it seemed over amped and still ridiculous.

Once again the gods just did not align to make a success. It may be a cult "hit" but it just does not make music for the masses.

~

Aspects of Love

Andres Lloyd Weber was being accused of not being able to write anything intimate and small. Everything he wrote was big, "Phantom", of course, "Starlight Express", "Cats" and he took the challenge.

Trevor Nunn directed this and it was based upon the novella of the same name it was a long dull boring musical soap opera and it was lackluster in many ways. It reinvented dull characters who bed hopped as the major interest in the musical.

The reviews were lackluster and *New York Times* critic

Frank Rich wrote in a negative review "Whether *Aspects of Love* is a musical for people is another matter."

When the musical closed, the entire $8 million investment was lost, which, according to the *New York Times*, made it "perhaps the greatest flop in Broadway history."

With the experts at the helm who have created two of the biggest hits that were running at the time the expectations were very high for this. This musical also started the trend that ALW was not continuing at the top of his game as he had yet to have again a big musical success.

~

Sunset Boulevard

Reflecting on this one, having seen it three times and the star turns of Glenn Close, Betty Buckley and also Diahann Carroll left an impression. All were incredible but in retrospect it was an over bloated attempt to make a musical out of a classic movie that maybe should have been left alone.

The movie of course with Gloria Swanson and William Holden became an instant classic for two reasons. One the people in it could have been real. The story could have been real at the time and the insult to the Hollywood machine was truly evident in the tone and very execution of the movie.

In 1950, the idea of an aging star keeping a younger man, she herself a recluse and castaway from Hollywood's dream machine was a very difficult story to tell. In its' day the silent film stars who were forgotten were real and a painful reality.

As a musical it had been looked at by Stephen Sondheim and Hal Prince as a vehicle for Angela Lansbury. Yet their vision was a book style musical not a totally sung through musical. The result, the project never went far.

Enter Andrew Lloyd Weber who thought it a great

opportunity after the "Phantom "success. It seemed almost to be a companion piece of sorts.

There is the well documented off stage drama as well with Patti Lupone cast as Norma and committed by contract to open the musical in New York, the opening in LA with Glenn Close, add Faye Dunaway into the mix as her replacement (getting fired) then Patti being ignored per her contract for the New York opening, so that Glenn Close could go to New York. There was enough bad behavior to write a new musical.

The show was over produced and bloated with a levitating set and all sorts of size components that made it costly to run. Then add in the Divas who had to be paid to star and you have a very expensive operation.

Sadly it is a small story and the overwhelming Broadway production added very little to enhance it. The challenge seems to be that when compared to the original this one pales by comparison. The original was a "real" story. The musical seemed pretentious and laden down by its very size.

It ran and was a success for the audiences, but it failed in terms of revenue and profit.

This should have worked after all it had 'Sir Andrew" and stellar cast, incredible sets. Acceptable music, but at the same time the story was "cultish" from an old movie and was not presented with current relevance.

If "Phantom of the Opera "could run forever, than why wouldn't this as well? The sheer size and needs of a star killed it.

~

Victor Victoria

Classic movies have not just recently become the idea for Broadway musicals. When you have a famous Broadway star that has not appeared on Broadway since 1960 then have a movie role she made famous, why not turn the movie into a Broadway musical? How can you lose?

First of all you keep the composer alive. Next you hope the ego of the writer (Blake Edwards) does not get into the way and then you set it in motion. The musical should have worked accept that Henry Manicini died and they enlisted Frank Wildhorne who never has written a successful musical to carry on. Julie Andrews with her glowing 4 octave range received great reviews, although the show did not. This was not the comedy that the movie was able to accomplish and what Blake Edwards could create in farce on screen seemed almost tame and dull on stage. It too was overshadowed by the attempted size.

It's not a bad musical but not a great one. Julie was nominated for a best actress award but withdrew her name when nothing nor anyone else from the musical was nominated at all.

She felt it disrespectful to the efforts of so many to be singled out for the one Tony nomination the show would receive.

No one involved would think that doing this project would end her singing career. Singing eight performances a week and having to sing in lower registers not suited to a coloratura Soprano wreaked havoc on her and she developed vocal nodes. The surgery she required ended her singing ability and she sued the surgeon and did win an enormous settlement, but was that worth the cost?

This is one that should have been a huge success, even when Liza Minelli took over; the show sagged with her presence. The attraction was the star, and it had a built in audience who loved the movie but that did not make the show outstanding and in fact may have led to it's over hyped demise.

It ran two years and was a respectable run at the time, yet the 1990's were not truly a creative time for musicals and "Victor Victoria" didn't do much to advance the genre. It could have been fantastic at the hands of a group who were more tuned into Broadway musicals.

~

Ragtime

Flaherty and Ahrens along with Terence McNally took the sprawling novel by E.L. Doctorow and created a musical that was lush, vibrant dramatic and huge! It told many stories at once and interspersed non fictional characters into the story.

The musical caught the sound of the "Rag" and had true vocal power and strength. It to some seemed bloated yet it was a terrific attempt at a fully sung musical of great power almost in the style of "Porgy and Bess" and "Showboat".

This further gave us Audra MacDonald, Brian Stokes Mitchell and Marin Mazzie, All luscious performers. Yet it was so big that it couldn't afford itself.

Then there was the scandal that may have had "accounting errors" which closed the show. It also was competing with "The Lion King" for recognition and the two shows were battling it out for the awards. To say which was better is mute as the Disney spectacle sure killed it, but "Ragtime" was formidable.

It is hard to say but the extravagant production may have just killed itself much like the case in"Sunset Boulevard". Bigger isn't always is better and the sprawling novel in text may have been overshadowed by the live action on stage that overshadowed the weaknesses in the script.

In any event this was not a hit, lost money and is so huge

that to do it today is not feasible. The recent revival was also a disaster.

Tarzan

Even Disney could screw up! You would think with their backlog of animated movies that they couldn't fail. Phil Collins wrote the music as he had written for the movie but no one seemed the least bit interested in what appeared on stage. It ran a year.

Well, Disney musicals are supposed to be blockbusters and run forever. Somehow this just did not click. Everything was going for it, sets that were beautiful, musical that was semi familiar for the movie fans and certainly an amiable cast. Yet even Disney can create a lackluster evening.

The "New York Times" decimated it, calling it "a giant green blob with music"

You can almost compare this to the Rodgers and Hammerstein " Allegro!". The third musical and not as good as the first two! This was Disney's third and following "The Lion King" what in the world could they do to that?

This was a sick cousin to the two musicals that preceded it and limped along for a year then closed.

15 Interesting Failures of Broadway Musicals Featuring Star Turns

- ☆ *Wildcat (Lucille Ball)*
- ☆ *Coco (Hepburn)*
- ☆ *Tovarich (Vivien Leigh)*
- ☆ *Miss Moffut (Bette Davis)*
- ☆ *I Had A Ball (Buddy Hackett)*
- ☆ *Take Me Along (Jackie Gleason)*
- ☆ *Jenny (Mary Martin)*
- ☆ *The Boy From OZ (Hugh Jackman)*
- ☆ *Little Me (Sid Caesar)*
- ☆ *Breakfast at Tiffany (Mary Tyler Moore and Richard Chamberlain)*
- ☆ *Happy Hunting (Merman)*
- ☆ *New Girl In Town (Verdon)*
- ☆ *Dear World (Angela)*
- ☆ *Mack and Mabel (Robert Preston)*
- ☆ *The Rink (Liza Minelli and Chita Rivera)*

Wildcat 1960

Lucille Ball the queen of television comedy after her divorce from Desi Arnaz decided that she needed to get her children out of California and seized upon the idea of doing the musical "Wildcat!" The project by N.Richard Nash had been envisioned for a much younger person but with Desilu financing the production and owning the recording rights, production control, and television rights it was Balls' show.

The show had luke-warm reviews. The audiences came expecting to see the Lucy character in a musical so over time the star shifted the character to emulate what her fans loved from television. Most of this was not consistent with the script and was not a helping to drive an audience to the show.

Even appearing on the Ed Sullivan Show, with Lucy singing "Hey Look Me Over ", was not a huge help.

Further she was ill and collapsed on stage forcing the producers close the show so the star could recover and then re-open it some weeks later. It became clear no Lucille Ball meant no audience as she was the reason people would fill the theatre. Further the musicians union fought for the orchestra to be paid during the closure and this battle closed the show permanently.

The reigning queen of television could not handle the demands of the Broadway musical and ultimately retreated back to her medium for her remaining career.

~

Coco 1969

Originally Freddie Brisson had optioned the idea of a musical based upon Coco Chanel for his wife Rosalind Russell but crippling arthritis made it impossible for her to consider the project. Alan Jay Lerner and Andre Previn had envisioned a musical about Coco Chanel for some time.

Another major star had to be found and Hepburn was convinced to give it consideration. She worked at the idea of singing with Roger Edens and determined with the right approach musically she could do it. Certainly if you listen to the Tony sequence with her doing the finale the idea was to make her sound like a female Henry Higgins.

Cecil Beaton created a technical nightmare of a set that created severe difficulties and the cast had to endure the Hepburn needs to keep the theater at 60 degrees at all times causing the cast to constantly be sick. Great stars have great demands.

The script was highly fictionalized and Chanel herself became more like an inspiration than an actual story. It ran because of Hepburn's fame which drove it. The show itself truly had received mediocre reviews. When she left the New York production to tour nationally, she was the draw, the Broadway production closed. It was also considered to be the most expensive musical ever to be produced at the time with a $900.000 price tag.

Paramount who had invested in the musical had the idea that it would become a motion picture, but they abandoned the idea.

~

Tovarich (Vivien Leigh) 1963

A musical based upon a classic Greta Garbo Movie seemed like a great idea!

When a musical opens and it is all based upon the name on the marquis it can become serious when the star falls ill and no one then has any interest. In the case of "Tovarich!" Vivien Leigh was in new territory in a musical and certainly she had the fame to break new ground starring in a Broadway Musical. She even won the Best Actress in a Musical Tony. But her personal mental health would not allow her to continue the role.

By this point in her career she was a well-worn

temperamental diva and made demands that made the production work difficult. She had bouts of depression and would always ask to be forgiven for the outbursts that seemed out of control.

Besides being Bi-polar she had terrible bouts with Tuberculosis and this impacted her ability to perform. Her need to stop performing the play forced its early closure. As good as she was her personal issues sunk the project.

It is too often the case as noted here star power can make or break a musical.

~

Miss Moffut (Bette Davis)

Just look at the star and the answer is clear. Can you really see Bette Davis leading in a musical?

~

I Had A Ball (Buddy Hackett)

This was a typical mistake in the theatre; you take a comic actor and package lots of shtick and hope it can become a musical. It was a series of routines that were short on book connection but were all there to showcase the comic genius of its star. Steven Suskin called this the "clown show"; "clown shows were about the fellow — almost always a man — at the center Ed Wynn, Bert Lahr, Victor Moore or the brothers Marx."

Upon opening the show had a robust review in Detroit but by the time it got to Broadway seemed to be a tired evening of comic antics, almost like a TV variety show with some themes of a plot thrown into connects the scenes. It ran a few months because of the star power of its lead at the time. Musically Hackett was challenged and numbers were cut as he just could not handle them.

The NY reviews were not enthusiastic Hackett to make it work looked for cameo appearances from friends to keep the audience engaged, but he went off book to try and make it even funnier and he seemed to tire of it and ultimately wanted out of his contract.

The new competition of "Hello Dolly" and "Funny Girl" over shadowed this early on and he saw that the show was not going to fare well against those. There was no idea of who to replace him with so the show ultimately closed. When it is star power that makes a show work and the star becomes frantic and disenchanted it is not fun for anyone.

~

Take Me Along (Jackie Gleason)

One has to look back in amazement sometimes what creative teams are thinking. A Eugene O'Neill play as a musical is a first wonder!

David Merrick who produced it was only in it half-heartedly and somewhat was annoyed that he had to promote Jackie Gleason over the play. This in fact was the challenge. Jackie Gleason live on Broadway became more important than what actually happened on the stage.

The musical was faithful to the coming of age story that O'Neil had created but still it all added up to only a star power evening with a major TV personality and overshadowed the story at hand. One could question the suitability of the material for musicalization in the first place.

It ran for a year and rarely has been seen since.

Jenny (Mary Martin)

The first word of advice most people give is never use your own money to finance a Broadway musical! Mary Martin ignored that and she and her husband financed this major disaster. It should have been a success based upon the pedigree involved. She had wanted to create a musical based upon Laurette Taylor, but did not want to use her friends name as the character. This seriously impacted the reality of what they tried to create. As a truly "biographical" (think "Funny Girl") piece it might have resonated far better with the audience.

This creative process was frustrating. It is a story of continual back stage bickering and the ensuing replacement of leadership and talent all of the way to Broadway. It was a battleground from Boston to Detroit and then back to New York. Lawsuits flared and it never helped create a solid musical entertainment.

The score was critically praised and Martins' comedic antics were found "charming" but there was little else to praise. Howard Taubman, in *The New York Times* wrote: "Not that Miss Martin has lost her luster...she continues to be a game and resourceful trouper, willing to do an impossible backbend while being carried aloft and game enough to let herself be whirled head over heels on a torture rack and come up smiling and belting out a top note"

Star power can only go so far if the vehicle is wrong.

~

The Boy From Oz (Hugh Jackman)

It is tough to put on a musical that has to feature a Judy Garland and a Liza Minelli in the story and not have a cartoonish atmosphere. The music written by the protagonist in this juke box bio created a semi ridiculous evening of musical theatre. However, you add to the mix the extraordinary star charisma of Hugh Jackman who to the delight of the audience took off his shirt twice during the performance gave a star power to an idiotic comic strip of a musical.

In reality it was just awful. Odd and none of it really worked as the story was so cliché ridden that it was laughable. Yet there was this huge talent in the lad who kept you engaged for the entire mess of what appeared around him.

The whole musical was forced and the music chosen really did not fit the action on stage. The reality of the singer/pianist/composer who married Liza Minelli (and he was actually gay) then died of AIDS just was not told in a way to be believable or emotionally engaging.

The NY Times was far from pleasant about the evening; it was Hugh Jackman that ultimately carried it forward into a Tony Award Winning performance. It was Jackman that enabled the show to recoup it $8.25 million investment but at the end his contract no one wanted to touch the role or the piece. You could say it was a success in that it recouped what was spent but when a musical dies at the end of its run and no one wishes to see it again you get the picture.

Watching it, you knew that Hugh Jackman was on the verge of major stardom.

"Little Me" Sid Caesar

For such an unsuccessful musical this musical has come up often here! Sid Caesar who with his major Television fame and taking with him his writer Neil Simon did not create a solid hit musical here. In truth it is far more entertaining than it was given credit for at the time.

The score by Cy Coleman had two hit songs on the radio to help its' success but the comic antics never caught on and Sid Caeser himself was most probably the problem as he was not in a good frame of mind to carry off the demands of a Broadway show 8 times a week.

This is another example of how "star power" can be damaged by the demons of the real person and can impact the run and profitability of a musical. He was a comic sketch artist and the musical was really a series of sketches. After his TV fame of ten years he had faded from the spotlight quickly and was a memory. His style here, almost a way to rekindle his TV persona did not linger long and sadly the image and the person he was collided here.

This was revived in the 1990's with Martin Short and the antics worked, it is not an outstanding musical however in the right hands it is a lot of fun.

~

Breakfast at Tiffany Mary Tyler Moore and Richard Chamberlain

You take a widely praised and beloved movie with an iconic theme song, then a few years after it is in theatres take two hugely popular television talents and you might have a hit. Then for great writing you add Abe Burrows who wrote terrific musical books, only to replace him with Edward Albee. The logic is just not present.

Morale among the cast was disastrous after Burrows was dismissed, yet the advance sale for the musical was huge, the names for the two stars alone sold tickets! The musical never opened and David Merrick took out a huge ad at the time. The ad announcing that he shut down the production, "rather than subject the drama critics and the public to an excruciatingly boring evening" was typical Merrick style.

The lack of Chemistry between the leads was truly evident. Mary Tyler Moore was the spirit and charisma of Audrey Hepburn. She may have had personality, but the comparisons were sure to be made. The story itself was a small intimate story of a free spirit recovering from her childhood of abuse, and her reality was not always on target. These were characters that could not survive a full musical treatment. It's often best to leave the glorious films alone.

~

Happy Hunting (Merman)

Ethel Merman had not had a big Broadway hit since "Call Me Madam", was now married and happily living in Colorado when her then husband the president of Continental Airlines pushed her to taking this project on as a way to give both her and his airline publicity.

The plot focuses on a Philadelphia Main Line widow and her efforts to find a royal husband for her daughter Beth. While in Monaco at the wedding of Princess Grace, they search. Merman never loved the project, and at first was pleased with co-star Fernando Lamas, but soon after rehearsals began they clashed. He publicly criticized her performance, and as tensions between them escalated, soon they stopped speaking to each other.

Lamas, certain he would be second fiddle to Merman, plotted to draw the focus away from her. According to various sources, he was known throughout Hollywood for his unusually large physical endowment. He instructed costume designer Irene Sharaff to cut his pants so they would cling as tightly as possible. On opening night in Philadelphia, his appearance elicited loud gasps from the audience when he stepped out on stage for the first time. Can you imagine??? Merman was not amused by the vulgar display and demanded his costume be altered—she was no shy individual and could curse like a truck driver—however the unprofessional behavior infuriated her.

She hated the score and kept asking for new music. She hated Lamas as well. The chemistry was just horrible. The advance sales were strong as after all it was a new Merman musical (much to the dismay of Lamas).

Merman got praise for her performance and lost the Tony award to Judy Holiday in "Bells are Ringing"

The show ran about a year and has rarely been seen or heard of since.

~

New Girl In Town (Verdon)

It is so hard to imagine a musical based upon Eugene O'Neill In the first place but to be based upon "Anna Christie" is even odder.

It had a lot going for it after all Freddie Brisson and Hal Prince produced it, Bob Fosse was going to choreograph it and Gwen Verdon was to star in it. That is a strong combination of potential success. Then you add on the master of George

Abbott writing the book and you would think he would have known what to do as well.

This is too tragic a story for the style of musical comedy in the 1950's. It was a gloomy play about a prostitute who wanted to change her life. As it was a musical the story ends with an upbeat ending which is not the exact O'Neill style.

The reviews were not ecstatic.

This was also created for Gwen Verdon who at this point in time had reached major acclaim after her stint in "Damn Yankees". She received great acclaim for her portrayal in this production too. The problem also was that Fosse who was hired to create great dance moments was involved in a musical that did not require that in the story.

It also was interesting that during its tryout the show was closed because of a lude dream ballet that Fosse created. It was a musical that had music that just did not fit the needs of a musical story line. The show was acclaimed at the time because of the star. The life of a former prostitute from an earlier era on stage in the late 1950's in a musical was far too "avant-garde" to be truly successful

~

Dear World (Angela Lansbury)

As noted previously this should have been a great success. Jerry Herman at the top of his acclaim having had two back to back successes and starring the leading lady who led a recent success for him should have made an incredible hit. It just was not to be. First of all the play the "Madwoman of Chaillot" is a stylish story full of symbolism. The focus on idealism, love and poetry rising over greed has values that are soaring but when put to music get complicated in its' vision.

It seemed that no one could make it work; that many

directors came and went did not help. The show never gelled. It was far too massive a musical for the small important sense of storytelling that was in the play. The musical became way to over weighted for the message. Symbolic stories just don't always translate well to musical treatment.

Angela Lansbury's acclaim could not even lift the musical to any success yet the music has certainly become a cult favorite.

~

Mack and Mabel (Robert Preston)

It is always interesting how a disaster of a musical came reach such cult status. This has been discussed in great detail earlier as well and once again the pedigree of Jerry Herman, Gower Champion and Michael Stewart re-uniting the "Hello Dolly!" team just couldn't rescue this story about two Hollywood legends.

Certainly Robert Preston was considered legendary and magical by this point of his career and to see him star in a musical would have been considered a strong moment of Broadway wonder. Yet the star power and the great creative team just could not make it happen.

The characters were too unlikable and the whole inconsistency of the story telling was also a victim of its producer losing interest (as was a common David Merrick trait). He gave up on it (maybe justifiably) and to this day this remains a personal favorite of Jerry Herman who felt it was abandoned by the whole creative team.

~

The Rink

Liza Minelli at the top of her fame and the mega Broadway name of Chita Rivera couldn't save this tale of mother daughter conflict. It was meant to be an intimate musical examining the relationship between and Italian American mother and her estranged daughter. It started with Arthur Laurents writing the book, to be replaced by Terence McNally and in place of an intimate musical it too became a bloated over produced inconsistent mess.

The Kander and Ebb score was not the best and Frank Rich of the New York Times called it "Turgid and sour" he felt the dialogue was banal and the characters ciphers. The attack was painful for Kander and Ebb who felt it was exactly as they had envisioned it and that the stars were attacked.

Such is what can happen when strong names are associated with a project that has little compassion. The production also closed when Liza Minnelli had to enter rehab.

21 Great Women's Star Turns in Musicals

- ☆ *Lauren Bacall Applause*
- ☆ *Gertrude Lawrence The King and I*
- ☆ *Ethel Merman Annie Get Your Gun*
- ☆ *Ethel Merman Call Me Madam*
- ☆ *Angela Lansbury Gypsy*
- ☆ *Angela Lansbury Sweeney Todd*
- ☆ *Mary Martin South Pacific*
- ☆ *Carol Channing Hello Dolly!*
- ☆ *Angela Lansbury Mame!*
- ☆ *Rosalind Russell Wonderful Town*
- ☆ *Gwen Verdon Damn Yankees*
- ☆ *Gwen Verdon Sweet Charity*
- ☆ *Vivian Blaine Miss Adelaide*
- ☆ *Patti Lupone Evita*
- ☆ *Ann Reinking Chicago*
- ☆ *Glenn Close Sunset Boulevard*
- ☆ *Elaine Strictch Company*
- ☆ *Alexis Smith Follies*
- ☆ *Bernadette Peters Sunday In The Park With George*
- ☆ *Bernadette Peters Gypsy*
- ☆ *Patti Lupone Gypsy*

Lauren Bacall Applause

As she herself announced, the most famous widow in Hollywood was taking a risk. When she was approached to star as the great character that was made famous by Bette Davis, Margo Channing, she was apprehensive as she knew she couldn't sing and she knew she couldn't dance. However, in 1970 her tour de force performance took a fair musical and made it truly raise the rafters. She reinvented her career once again and now was a star in all of performing the media. "Applause" in its day seemed like a great entertainment but it was the star power of Lauren Bacall that made it exceptional. The story was familiar as noted earlier, based loosely on the movie "All About Eve" (which was not able to be used as the basis of the musical) but rather the novel that preceded it was. The result was a 1970 contemporary style of story which makes it very dated today stylistically.

Lauren Bacall was truly one who possessed great stage presence and it showed. Her charm, her charisma, her great sense of character and style truly crossed the footlights. If you listen to a recording of "Applause", she in her way out did Bette Davis and gave the role of Margo Channing a great new presentation. This is also an example of take the star out of the role and you don't get much after.

~

Gertrude Lawrence The King and I

As discussed earlier here as well. the well-known diva of her day was not known for her great signing or her personal charm. She was a woman who set fashion, had style and was known for eating people alive.

Having read "Anna and the King of Siam" and having seen the Rex Harrison/ Irene Dunne movie she believed it was a perfect musical vehicle for her. She came to meet with Rodgers and Hammerstein who were not sure they wanted to be involved with the diva she was known to be and even more did not see the potential of where a musical in the style they liked to write would come from.

There was no traditional love story and they knew that

the character Lawrence wanted to play would not be the love interest. However after great pleading from her they found a way to create the musical that would become 'The King and I". Many reviews of her performance were very polite, and she was praised for not eating the scenery. Yet she was the star that made it happen.

~

Ethel Merman—"Annie Get Your Gun"

You take Brassy Ethel, add a musical with oversized characters based upon real life figures from the Wild West and you had "Annie Get your Gun". Irving Berlin who came late to the project after the sudden death of Jerome Kern wrote musical numbers for Ethel that shook the rafters.

As noted earlier, in 1966 she revived her legendary performance, and yes due to her age it was nicknamed "Granny Get Your Gun" but it was terrific to see Ethel Merman do her thing! Hearing her sing "You Can't Get a Man With a Gun" or "You Got the Sun in the Morning or the Moon At Night" was still a thrill. Annie Oakley was never a great character, not honestly written drama or sophistication yet what a fun part. Ethel Merman had her style of performance and it was what it was. She played to the balcony and reached the theatre across the street with her voice. She was iconic and to have seen her create or re-create the role was an artistic moment. She knew what to do and did to well.

Ethel Merman Call Me Madam

Irving Berlin had found his golden diva with Merman and after his next musical "Miss Liberty" flopped the idea of getting involved with Merman again must have made sense.

A real life Democratic Party fundraiser Pearl Mesta had been appointed ambassador to Luxemburg and this was the basis of the political satire that became "Call Me Madam". A satire on politics and foreign affairs it also spoofed America's penchant for lending billions of dollars to needy countries. The story focused on a great "friend" of President Truman a well-meaning but naïve socialite who is appointed to the fictional European country of Lichtenburg as Ambassador. While there, she charms the local gentry, and complications ensued.

It was Merman at her brassy best. As usual Merman called the shots making numbers get cut, and adding new ones, but she was the center of a situation comedy show. This was her great ability to perform.Merman was like no one else and to see her perform music written just for her on a satire built around her was a great performance to catch.

~

Ethel Merman 'Gypsy"

After the musical disaster of "Happy Hunting" she needed a hit. Arthur Laurents who created the interest in the biography of Gypsy Rose Lee had wanted to have Stephen Sondheim to write the words and music. Ethel who was seriously reeling from her disaster in "Happy Hunting" was not going to allow someone who never wrote words and music for a new musical do this to her again. She insisted on Jule Styne and Stephen Sondheim of course wrote the wonderful lyrics.

To the surprise of all involved Ethel was shaping up to deliver a powerful performance in what would be hailed by many to be the greatest part ever written for the musical theatre for a woman. Ethel was a triumph giving the part the performance of her career and of course no one in the audience missed a word of the wonderful lyrics that were created.

Ethel Merman solidified her presence in the crown of the great musical performers of the American stage.

~

Angela Lansbury Gypsy

As noted earlier here, in 1973 there was a London production planned of "Gypsy" as it had never been performed in London. The original Mama Rose of choice was to be Elaine Stritch but thickets were not selling so Angela Lansbury was cast and they fired poor Elaine. There was great concern that the shadow Ethel Merman on stage would always a hunt any actress who would try to create the role on stage.

Angela created a different character for her version of Mama Rose. She had a bitter elegance that Ethel could not possess, she was aching for the success of having a daughter became a star, the dream she had for herself but would never attain. Her performance was so applauded by critics that she brought the revival to Washington, DC and to New York to great praise.

Were it not for this performance no other star of the day might have tackled the role in major productions. Angela set the sun on Ethel's embodiment of the role and opened the vison of a different sort of Mama Rose for others.

~

Angela Lansbury Sweeney Todd

This is not everyone's favorite musical, but certainly one of mine. The twinkling in the eye of Angela Lansbury as Mrs. Lovett is unforgettable. Her comic timing added to the scariness and depravity of the role made it watchable.

Watching Angela pound dough while singing the tongue twisting lyrics to "The Worst Pies in London"—alone was a feat! She then truly almost impersonates the devil throughout her time on stage yet, being lovable all at the same time. It was impossible but Angela created a comic character out of a character that could not be likable of lovable at all.

She once again proved that she was the reigning first lady of the musical theatre. Having seen her do this twice live and then again and again in the DVD with George Hearn it was a masterful performance.

What makes Sweeney watchable is the coy, sly, impish charm Angela gave to a totally dislikable character.

~

Mary Martin South Pacific

Well OK, I never saw her do the part (wasn't even born yet), and frankly I have a hard time thinking Mary Martin was as wonderful as those who saw her recall but she created a part that had innocence, charm, real growth, and caring. The part is so well written both in words and music that any solid actress can take it on.

Listen to the recording of her, it may still be hard to imagine! Yet reputation does have something to say for it. After she signed on she was worried that she could never sing a duet and be heard with Ezio Pinza and begged the team to not write any duets for them. They agreed and the part is written without any duets. It was a different sort of writing. What Mary Martin brought to the role was a charming innocence that was her perky stage presence.

There are early TV films of her performing some of the songs and at the time she was applauded with great raves. Why argue, one has to really say that Mary Martin set a bar fairly high as Nellie Forbush.

~

Carol Channing " Hello Dolly!"

Carol Channing is not to be understood from a record— after all what do you even hear? That voice of a frog almost. Yet on stage she had a sparkle that you could see vividly in the last row of the second balcony and a stage presence and charm that was contagious.

She made this her character and even though the part was envisioned for Merman, made it hers to own. Mary Martin turned it down as well, and the result was Channing created a legend. She owned the part so much that she played it forever.

It is hard to imagine how she beat out Barbra Streisand for a Tony, yet she was the known commodity at the time that was to be rewarded. There is also the reported feud between the two stars when Barbra got the ill-gotten movie, where she and Walter Matthau were as ill-suited as one can imagine. Channing begged for the part but it was her being in "Thoroughly Modern Millie" that convinced the team behind the movie that they did not like the way she looked on screen so the part went elsewhere.

Channing however set a level of performance for all stage Dolly's to match.

Ironically when Dolly and Channing became the successes they became, Mary Martin was the first to throw her hat into the ring to do the part next and she did the London production and toured it.

Channing however still owned the part even though many over the hill actresses took it on. They were never Channing. Merman may have been the only one to top her, but Channing owned the part. There may have been 7 Broadway Dolly's but Channing was the one.

~

Angela Lansbury Mame!

When the idea of creating a musical out of the wonderful "Auntie Mame" play/movie, the search for 'Auntie Mame "began. Who would take it on? They of course wanted Rosalind Russell but that was not going to happen. They wanted Lucille Ball next and she wasn't leaving television to tackle Broadway again.

The team kept looking and Jerry Herman who must have seen Angela in the ill-fated "Anyone Can Whistle" had the idea that Angela Lansbury might be perfect. He personally coached her for her backers audition and of course she won the part.

That was the reinvention of a career. Angela, of course became the toast of Broadway." Life Magazine" cover and all of the acclaim that would go with it. She even said at a New York Times theatre weekend interview that it was a heady experience walking down the street and having every one whistle at you. The musical is what it is a rework of a very good movie, that isn't really as good as the source. It was her performance that made it become legendary. Never since has there been a "Mame" as wonderful as she was. There were imitations and others who took on the part but it was never what Angela gave it.

~

Rosalind Russell Wonderful Town

Freddie Brisson knew his wife needed to be re-invented. Her career in Hollywood was somewhat washed up and her kind of character and style as not of current roles. He knew her old movie 'My Sister Eileen" and that when Bernstein, Comden and Greene began the project he made sure that his wife was married to the part. Bernstein knew that Roz had a very limited range and wrote comic music for Russell to sing. A part was created that give her the ability to have great comic timing in a new arena—a musical.

The New York Times was so enthusiastic for her portrayal that they claimed she could run for president and win based upon her performance. This was a career re-inventing role and as a result reignited her film stardom.

There was a television version done in the late 1950's you can catch some of the magic on YouTube.

~

Gwen Verdon Damn Yankees

This was a first major role for Gwen Verdon. She had made a breakthrough of course in "Can-Can but her husband Bob Fosse choreographed her to stardom. Her version of "Whatever Lola Want's became a famous sexy siren song that was a show stopper.

The part itself isn't the greatest character ever written and others have tried it but it is still the property of Gwen Verdon. To see her energy, the movie does catch it, but a wonderful scene in the movie is the song "Who's Got the Pain" a song she actually dances with her husband Bob Fosse. Catch it on YouTube. It shows the master and his muse fully delivering the style that made them both famous.

~

Gwen Verdon Sweet Charity

Star power rescued and made a musical a dancing legend. The musical itself isn't the greatest, the score has elevated it as discussed earlier, but as a theater piece take away the dancing and it is a bit of a bore. Gwen Verdon created a tour de force supported by two great dancing sidekicks. Over time this has been accepted as a great Broadway Classic.

Yet Gwen Verdon in 1966 was the top of the Broadway star pack. The musical itself did not get great reviews but her tireless intensity danced itself over the spotlights and she was the champion and embodiment of the Fosse style and legend.

To validate the excellence of what she could deliver search YouTube Gwen Verdon "I'm a Brass Band" or any other number from the show and settle in for a treat. It is hard to sometimes imagine the legends but you can still see it live as millions did then.

~

Vivian Blaine Miss Adelaide

Sometimes a part can eat you alive.

Vivian Blaine became a house hold name playing Miss Adelaide the long time fiancé of Nathan Detroit in "Guys and Dolls". She got raves for her performance and was even given the movie. It just stuck with her and no matter what else she did she was always Miss Adelaide. The lament that Frank Loesser wrote for the character is one of the most famous musical numbers ever written for a Broadway Musical and it was a showstopper among showstoppers in "Guys and Dolls".

She set the bar and maybe others have followed but she is still branded as the original.

It was considered a great classic performance; this too can be seen on YouTube.

~

Patti Lupone Evita

To hear Patti Lupone tell it, she churlishly says this was a tough experience as the part was so vocally demanding. Yet to become a major star because of a part and then put it in a category that one has to moan about it is odd.

However, seeing her Eva Peron was a major piece of artistry at the time. She was engrossing in the part believable and truly in command as a young performer getting her big chance.

It is not an easy part and the multimedia extravaganza that Hal Prince created for her was a tough piece of theatrics to stand up to. Yet she was able to rise above the great style around her and create a character that was not totally likable, driven and certainly tragic. There was an engagement to all of her performance that put the charisma beyond the footlights.

~

Ann Reinking Chicago 1996

To take on the shadow of Gwen Verdon must have been tough but it is Ann Reinking who masterminded the choreography and the style of the Fosse work and re-created it for the revival of "Chicago" that is still running 19 years later.

Being a protégé of the great master and not to mention a major romantic interest does create a certain ability to channel the exact pulse of the master. The pulse of the piece was understood and the unique approach to the story as reset in this revival is pure genius and masterful. The master himself would have been proud.

She channeled but did not copy her famous star that proceeded her 20 years earlier and made this her own but certainly caught the style perfectly. Her commitment to do justice to the Fosse style truly cannot be forgotten,

~

Glenn Close Sunset Boulevard

With all of the scandal that was associated with the part it was certainly something to see Glenn Close creep her way through the Andrew Lloyd Weber work. To take on a famous role in a movie and then add music to the character in totally sung form was daunting, not to mention she had to certainly overcome the nasty rumor mongering that came with it as she took over the part that was allegedly Patti Lupones'.

She was ghost like, spooky, tragic and pitied. A frail young woman who's fans had left her only to be misled about reality for years, becoming a recluse and then a tragic heroine in her real life. The part had huge shoes to fill as after all the memory of Gloria Swanson creating the very realistic Norma

Desmond is so famous a character, inevitable comparisons between performers would occur.

One advantage to the musical it is an acting performance about a distant character. It has to be truly performed. In the original the character was seemingly real as were those that surrounded her.

Glenn Close sang the part masterfully, became the sellout the musical needed as she created the famous character Norma Desmond and gave her bravura performance to the rafters. It's not a musical that may be among the greatest but the portrayal was certainly legendary.

It is an achievement that she was actually bigger than the set.

~

Elaine Strictch Company

The part was not a lead role, more of an ensemble character part in the cast. In a musical that was almost a series of skits on marriage, she had two songs the first "The Little Things You Do Together" which satirizes the games that couples do play together with each other. The other masterful song became her insignia. "The Ladies Who Lunch" the bitter song of an unhappy, bored, blasé, Upper East Side matron was delivered with a sardonic wit and style that set the show as it starts to wind down.

The performance was legendary and everyone who takes on the role is compared to the way Elaine Stritch sang this. If you aren't sure that the legend exists watch the DVD of the 80th Sondheim Birthday Celebration and see what happens when someone else sings the famous signature piece with Elaine sitting there watching.

Better yet watch the filming of the "Company" recording

on DVD and see the anguish she has as she can not a get a good recording of the number and the pain she endures trying to deliver it for the ages on vinyl.

It clearly elevated her status as a top tier Broadway performer and major interpreter of the Sondheim style and lyric.

~

Alexis Smith Follies

Take a faded "B-movie" queen and add the fantastic lyrics that Sondheim gave her to sing with Hal Prince's impeccable direction and then Alexis Smith became legendary once again. She had frequently acted and toured with her husband Craig Stevens, but her fame was truly faded, not quite as has been but certainly not star power. She took on the role of the Upper East Side matron married to the diplomat in "Follies", got glowing reviews and won a Tony for best actress. This too was legendary as no one really knew she could sing. Her stylish performance as the character Phyllis truly led the production. It was odd as the real lead seemed to be her counterpart Dorothy Collins, but when it all came down to the finish line Alexis Smith with her stylish performance stole the show.

Her rendition of "The Story of Lucy and Jessie" was a special tour de force, low key fizz and fierce.

Either of the two women in "Follies" are great roles but Alexis Smith created a legend.

Bernadette Peters "Sunday in the Park with George"

Of course a pointillist would have a girlfriend named DOT!

Then to have an actress who looks as if she actually came from the era and looks like the woman on the painting is pretty incredible. This performance solidified her as the great interpreter of Sondheim music and the parts they come from.

She utilized the tricky lyrics with precision and in addition easily played a 90-year old woman in the second act with grace and charm. This led her to the top of Broadway personalities in the recent era. Some parts seem to be able to be handled by almost anyone, yet Bernadette is such a classic performer that her initial interpretations of the Sondheim women are always the benchmarks,

This is a demanding role, having to play two distinct age ranges and be believable as well as wise; yet she took the bar lifted and made it for all others to follow in the piece. YOU can see her performance on DVD.

~

Bernadette Peters Gypsy

Truly unfair to her ability, people kept wondering, could she do it. Why would anyone wonder if she could do it of course she could?

Vocally she was outstanding, giving a unique charm to the monster of Mama Rose. She added a quality to the role that had always been missing—a sexuality that never was evident in the character. After all she had been married four times! Bernadette gave the role a truly sexy portrayal and she was terrific.

As an actress you can't be recognized as a champion of the Broadway musical until this role is tackled with success.

Sadly the Broadway gossip mongers tried to dispel her terrific performance but it was dynamic and charismatic in ways the predecessors never did.

Seeing her do "Roses Turn" as was done on the Tony awards of that year demonstrated the unique approach she took to the role. It had the usual passion and energy, but there was that vulnerability that hid just below the surface. The musical interpretation was softer as well which helped create the power the part so easily conveys.

~

Patti Lupone Gypsy

Gutsy, brash, and engaging all describe the approach Patti Lupone has taken to every role she tackles. Subtle would not be a word used to describe her style.

The rumor was that Arthur Laurents had complete control over who performed the role of Mama Rose in a full-fledged Broadway production. The rumor was that he had a feud going with Patti (although in her book she says not). She took the role in Ravinia in Illinois and achieved great reviews and acclaim performing it. The City Center of NYC in the summer Encores! Schedule added "Gypsy" with her in the lead. It received very strong reviews.

After this performance, evidently Arthur Laurents having seen it decided that the Broadway revival with Patti Lupone should occur after all and as a result Patti took on the role in a Broadway venue. It was a milestone as once again Broadway powerhouse performers should tackle the role. It was so soon after the recent revival with Bernadette Peters that many wondered—was it worth the bother so soon?

She achieved a great success adding her style to the part as well as those that had preceded her.

12 Roles to Be Cautious to Take On

- ☆ *Tony – West Side*
- ☆ *Mame*
- ☆ *Norma Desmond*
- ☆ *Henry Higgins*
- ☆ *Juan Peron*
- ☆ *The King of Siam*
- ☆ *Anything played by Hugh Jackman*
- ☆ *Maria – West Side*
- ☆ *Anything in The Lion King, Beauty and the Beast, Aladdin or anything in a Disney Musical*
- ☆ *Herbie in Gypsy*
- ☆ *Lancelot*
- ☆ *Fanny Brice, Nick Arnstein*

Tony – West Side Story

This is a part that propels the story but the character itself is not truly developed very well. The entire musical is truly an ensemble piece where the entirety creates the mood and the musical is the star not the lead character. The lead of the piece is the dance and the music. The actors are truly just the vehicle for what surrounds them into a great piece of musical theatre. The roles are rather flat.

The music that Tony sings is wonderful, challenging (try singing Maria the way it is actually written) and evokes the images that Bernstein, Sondheim and Arthur Laurents tried to create out of Romeo and Juliet.

Yet the male lead here is just a flat character that is the

mechanism for the story that evolves. He is a catalyst but not in control of the situation and although musically the story and the character get told he isn't the central player of the story. Instead in "West Side" it is the gangs as a unit that makes the character not the individuals. Tony is a naïve flat line. He is a victim of the story.

~

Mame

This is a wonderful character yet the dimensions required to be madcap, stylish, loving, mothering and zany is difficult for one actress to accommodate. The characteristics are many! It's all needed for the role or it doesn't convey. There has to be a subtle spin to make it really work.

Frankly since Angela Lansbury took the role and set the benchmark there has never been another person who can pull it off as well. Many have tried, including Ginger Rogers, if you can imagine, but the play can come off lifeless if the lead is less than charismatic beyond belief. It takes more than comic timing and having seen even Christine Baranski tackle the part recently it comes off somewhat flat. She had the free spirit basis, required but not the sparkle to make it really zing.

It is a tough role, as Mame has to have a charismatic oomph that can be grounded yet at the same time she must have a sincere determination that makes her totally believable and lovable. She is the Aunt we all wish we had.

The idea that a free spirited woman suddenly takes on her nephew who has been orphaned has to be so completely warmly developed while the free spirit of the person comes though—that is not easy. Part of the challenge is that the character of the play and movie that Rosalind Russell created is far better drawn than the character created in the musical.

The musical waters down the madcap style the character must have, yet it can be an elegant sophisticated role but it's risky to tackle.

~

Norma Desmond

I'm not sure why anyone would want to do this. First of all you are comparing yourself immediately to a legend in time. The Norma Desmond of the original film has almost become a real life legend. The character is so familiar to those who know the story that taking this on almost seems that you are conjuring up the dead. It's as if Norma Desmond was real.

It is a difficult, ghoulish sort of a role. The actress has to be sympathetic somewhere and even though she is keeping a young man for her personal desires as well as hoping to recapture the life of her youth it isn't easy to portray. She can easily be seen as a villain, but she needs to be seen as a pathetic, once somewhat likable and fragile, that has gone terribly astray.

Musically, although she hangs over the entire proceedings she isn't the biggest role in the piece (which is ironic) Joe Gillis is the far larger role dramatically as it is more his story. Yet her persona looms everywhere.

Playing Norma now is acting out a story that could have been real at the time of the original. Set up as you see it today, it is just a story The actress taking the part then has to imitate a time and person that is today hard to imagine. IN 1950 when the story was new it could have easily been real. Now it is a recollection of an era.

~

Henry Higgins

Is there any other way to portray this than the way Rex Harrison created it?

Having seen a few interesting Higgins actors (including Richard Chamberlain) and a recent actor at Arena Stage in DC who actually sang the notes in the Higgins songs was jarring. Talk about an alarming sound as the songs are so familiarly spoken to rhythm, that it is hard to watch someone else do this. Higgins and Rex became one over time as many have documented. Other actors who have followed have a tough road ahead.

Imagine when Hugh Jackman is a few years older than he is now he might make a wonderful Henry Higgins. He would create a new sensibility to the role which is so identified with what the one recollection everyone measures it to. This too familiar a role has expectations that are very clear when one enters the theatre. That expectation makes it very difficult to tackle. The classism and disrespect for British social mores have to be sarcastically portrayed in this part and his disregard for people other than himself has to be very clear.

It is not a simple part to play.

Juan Peron

Talk about being a second banana!

The whole story is about his wife and he has to hang around and try not to look bored or disinterested. The actor also can't seem wooden and if you read the history (if you can believe the musical is even close to anything accurate) must have been a pretty cunning and sly guy. He always seems to come off as manipulated by her and as a result he comes off almost buffoonish weak and sounding a bit like count sore throat pain if you recall those ads.

Anyone who tackles this one should now they are not going to be the actor that the audiences recall. That belongs to CHE in this piece.

~

The King of Siam

Well if you wish to emulate Yul Brynner you go down in hurry, and who else do you emulate to create.

The recent revival starring Ken Wattanabe certainly created a new and important take (and rumors were they had to work on his English a lot), but some legends just take on their own lives and this is a tough role to develop when the presence of the originator is so deeply connected to the role. Yul Brynner played the King 4500+ times over thirty years and many saw that performance not to mention the film. The character has wisdom and passion yet understands there are many things he does not understand. That and to be King is a very formidable character.

In the early vision of the role Rodgers and Hammerstein struggled with how to make the King sound real and not a silly accented character As a result the King comes off truly as a well regraded sympathetic character even though his philosophies are not truly those that one would agree with.

To tackle this and not be a cartoon, an impersonator or having a full head of hair, would be difficult. The expectations are set for the part and it is legendary in its creation.

~

Anything played by Hugh Jackman

He has not created that many Broadway roles but evidence enough was after his embodiment of Peter Allen no one would consider following him in the role. The guy oozes charisma charm and honest warmth. Having seen his one man show and other Broadway performances, he is absolutely incredible in his approach to a part. He engages you with his first smile!

Just know that if you have the chance to ever follow a part he created run as you will never be as good as him.

~

Maria – West Side

This is the parallel to Tony In the same piece. Maria is not well drawn, not that interesting, and suffers from being the female counterpart to the guy who gets killed in the end.

Her music is very virginal, she sings two songs and the second is a passionate plea for understanding from her friend Anita. She is the crux of the plot, but not a character that is deeply enough drawn to be truly interesting.

Read what was written above Tony and apply it here.

Her songs are even less interesting, "I Feel Pretty" is her only real solo and "One Hand One heart" is a bit schmaltzy. It is rumored that Sondheim hated this song and that he thought it was awful and Bernstein cried every time he heard it.

Who knows! The part is a flat line ingénue with not much to do but propel that story. Again the gangs are the story and she is just the mechanical piece.

Anything in" The Lion King", "Beauty and the beast", "Aladdin" or anything in a Disney Musical

Disney created a brand that clearly would not be defined by actors but rather by the brand itself. The reality is the brands are all good ones and rake in money for the Disney machine, but for an actor to be cast in any of the pieces certainly will not get them recognized for their talent and contribution to the entertainment or singled out. Imagine you've been a musical theatre major at a great school and get cast as a giraffe in "The Lion King". Yes you are working but, is that going to get you where you wish to truly go as an actor?

Not trying to be a snob here about working in a Disney musical, but going into a one is really somewhere that might not be a great career move unless it's just about a paycheck.

~

Herbie in Gypsy

What does any actor gain by playing this part? He is not the central character, and doesn't even sing anything other than a few lines here and there.

It is truly a part written for a weak man and that is what there is. Not much.

Herbie is just at tag along in the musical, a character that gets discarded along the way by his love Mama Rose. Although he is a catalyst of angst and sadness, and unfulfilled relationships in the story he is a mouse. Playing Herbie can't be a lot of fun.

~

Lancelot

What a dull role.

You first of all have to sit around backstage for about an hour while Arthur and Guinevere meet, then set up the round table talk and fall in love. Then you enter and sing this song 'C'est Moi" about how terrific you are. You are required to feign a French accent speaking English. Then add to that, try not to be wooden, try to look like you can sword fight and at the same time you must be an incredible baritone to save your credibility. After all you do get to sing a famous beautiful love song in Act II "If Ever I Would Leave You".

The part does not have a lot of real meat, and the love affair you are supposed to be having is oddly constructed. Then you are having a battle with Arthur over honor, it's all a bit odd, poorly created in the script and boring.

It isn't fun as it is a very one dimensional portrayal in a play that isn't very good to begin with. Its fame is not related to its real success at all and the recollection of "Camelot" is far better than its reality.

You will have fun singing the great famous love song and the audience will swoon, but frankly it is really not fun.

~

Fanny Brice, Nick Arnstein

Just be advised no one has tackled this onstage in a major way since the original in 1964. Imagine, if Streisand said she was going to do this on Broadway today we'd all go and she is in her 70's! It is just so connected to her that no one can be compared positively. So if this is a community theatre option and you take the part if you can sing like crazy things will probably work out. Just beware you will still be compared.

In a big production it is most probably unrevivable and it is a really good piece. Maybe Idina Menzel could do it (even though logically she is too old) or Lea Michelle. But "Funny Girl" is owned by its originator and taking it on makes you into instant comparison of why you are not her.

The male role, is so dull and uninteresting that to take that on you would have to be really desperate to do something. He sings a couple of side duets with the lead character but is not much pf a part either. Besides the musical is not about him anyway! He is window dressing period.

This is probably one of the most successful musicals from the 1960's and it is just impossible to revive. No one can match what it was.

Even singing the music from this is risky as it is so connected with its' famous star. Even the roles of Merman are far more approachable than this!

18 Great Audition Songs for Women

A few myths to consider never sing Sondheim. Why? That is just wrong. This list has music that is not always heard at auditions and might make someone look very original.

For years voice teachers have asked for ideas for young female students who go on auditions. The idea in an audition is to get remembered, do something that may be only 16 bars and make a powerful enough impression.

- ☆ *I Enjoy Being A Girl (Flower Drum Song)*
- ☆ *Dance Ten, Looks Three (A Chorus Line)*
- ☆ *Ballad Of Jenny (Lady In The dark)*
- ☆ *Losing My Mind (Follies)*
- ☆ *The Story of Lucy and Jessie (Follies)*
- ☆ *I Cain't Say No (Oklahoma)*
- ☆ *At The Library (She Loves Me)*
- ☆ *Glitter and Be Gay (Candide)*
- ☆ *The Worst Pies in London (Sweeney Todd)*
- ☆ *I Hate Men (Kiss Me Kate)*
- ☆ *So in Love (Kiss Me Kate)*
- ☆ *Gooches' Lament (Mame)*
- ☆ *If He Walked Into My Life (Mame)*
- ☆ *The Music That Makes Me Dance (Funny Girl)*
- ☆ *The Gentleman Is A Dope (Allegro)*

- ☆ *Bauble Bangles and Beads (Kismet)*
- ☆ *Another Hundred People (Company)*
- ☆ *I Get a Kick Out of You (Anything Goes)*

I Enjoy Being A Girl (The Flower Drum Song)

Rodgers and Hammerstein wrote great female songs, and this one if done correctly, with the syncopations and great lyrics about female sexuality and ego make a wonderful song to sell oneself at an audition. The lyrics are perky and lend themselves to fun interpretation and enable a character to shine through in a great, not often heard song. This sells confident womanhood. By the way it is a great audition song for a guy for "La Cage Aux Folles"

~

Dance Ten, Looks Three (A Chorus Line)

"A Chorus Line" was startling in its day and this is a great song for a belter that will keep you getting noticed. The more familiar name is "Tits and Ass" because of the story of how the singer bought them, and is the ribald song about how a dancer went the plastic surgery route to get the body she needed to get a role. It takes guts and determination to sell it, will enable a more demure looking performer to come across in a strong way. It is a brave song to sing at an audition but one that could easily work to an advantage, and the director will for sure recall who you are.

~

The Saga Of Jenny (Lady In the dark)

What is this one, never heard of it?

Well if you have ever listened to 'Follies" Sondheim copied styles from composers of an earlier era. His song" Story of Lucy and Jesse" emulates what Kurt Weill wrote for "Lady In the Dark" a piece called the "Ballad of Jenny" where she sings about not being able to make up her mind. It truly is great song that rarely gets heard today and if you wish to emulate a Sondheim Style from a different composer this could be a great piece. If you need to see it done, there is a YouTube video of it by Julie Andrews in the movie 'Star"

~

Losing My Mind (Follies)

Oh how torchy!!!!!

Again from "Follies" one of the great torch songs ever, with such a sad twist of agony. Some say you just don't audition with Sondheim; one does not have to agree. Yet if the audition might require a tragic sense of yearning this could really be the piece.

~

The Story of Lucy and Jessie (Follies)

Another gem from "Follies", see the notes above about the "Ballad of Jenny". This too is really a great, audition piece. Rarely do people use it, but if you shy away from Sondheim as many think you should try this one. The wit and sarcasm along with the bitterness could be a terrific selling point for the actor taking this piece on. The hidden bitterness that gets conveyed is wonderful to create in song and this too is an upbeat treasure.

~

I Cain't Say No (Oklahoma)

The trick to Rodgers and Hammerstein is to deliver it exactly as written. Rodgers wrote the music to emphasize the language and people sadly murder it all of the time. He wrote the rhythms for a reason and this discipline needs to be adhered to—exactly. To show true artistry if you do the piece in correct rhythm patterning it shows you off even better. This is a wonderful audition song for a character part and has all of the oomph that could position a singer with a comedic sense.

~

At the Library (She Loves Me)

Looking to show off a coloratura range wow this is a great one. From the musical "She Loves Me". It has great character work in it, a terrific range to show off and has all of the wonderful vocal range a belter soprano would want to show off and a great character song.

~

Glitter and Be Gay (Candide)

Among the most complicated songs that Bernstein ever wrote, but to show off your coloratura, with a big wow, this is killer.

It is ambitious as the syncopations are absolutely among the most difficult ever written for a musical. Add to it the tortuous high notes, and there is the package! If you are not confident in your rhythm you will kill it; however if savoir faire is your thing and you have the confidence to deliver in a big way, if you have killer ambition to show off you skill, this is it. Every young soprano should tackle it at least once.

~

The Worst Pies in London (Sweeney Todd)

It's another Sondheim piece. Why in the world??

Well it's a song of great rhythm, outstanding lyrical lines and great comedy. It is a terrific character song and frankly fits almost any female range. It is not too low, not too high and gives a singer a wide range of choices in delivery. Be warned the lyrics (as in all of Sondheim are the key). They have to be perfectly executed to the rhythm they were written to.

~

I Hate Men (Kiss Me Kate)

Cole Perter wrote a great variety of music but using the lyrics of Shakespeare and setting them to contemporary song was really genius. This is a terrific piece of music for a Broadway belter. The lyrics, you can't beat them. They are naughty, sophisticated and truly almost wicked fun to deliver. This is a song that can really set the singer apart. It calls for a great high note belter range, but wow! It is rarely heard as well.

~

So in Love (Kiss Me Kate)

Another romantic gem from "Kiss Me Kate". It is romantic, lush, contemporary and just beautifully singable. The piece enables a singer to use their high notes beautifully and yet croon about the lovely lower register music. It is true Cole Porter witty, sophisticated, stylish romantic lyrics and lush melody. It has real range and power, angst and emotion.

~

Gooches' Lament (Mame)

If you need comic intent, and need to present real vocal prowess this could be a great choice. It comes from "Mame" and has a huge range. This gives the singer great lyrics and comic approaches to put over, and a true opportunity to become riotous. It was a show stopper when originally performed as it is so comic and requires true vocal range. This too can be a great choice for a character part audition.

~

If He Walked Into My Life (Mame)

Another song from "Mame" this is a sad melancholy beautiful piece. It is an acting song about loss, love, hope and fear. It has anger, but has a warmth that when sung beautifully can be a tug on the heart strings. Go for it! It is just beautiful and will give the singer the ability to convey true depth of emotion in very honest ways.

~

The Music That Makes Me Dance (Funny Girl)

Why would anyone sing a Streisand song for gosh sakes?

Well it isn't either of the two biggies from "Funny Girl" and was written because they needed something that sounded like "My Man" as the original was not used in the score.

It is a beautiful song that has charm, yearning and desire. It is a slow ballad that builds. The song shows off range and skill, phrase control and character. It is not the most famous song from "Funny Girl" so tackling it should not be to challenging as a comparison.

~

The Gentleman is a Dope (Allegro)

There are a lot of Rodgers and Hammerstein pieces that are not all that famous.

This is one from "Allegro" and has great wit, scorn, satire, and as most songs should work as a one act play. It is a terrific song about a guy who doesn't get it. This is a mid-range piece and as with all of the Rodgers and Hammerstein pieces the rhythm is the thing. You get to be witty, clever 'nasty" and perplexed. All of these are great things to present emotionally in an audition piece.

~

Bauble Bangles and Beads (Kismet)

Show off your coloratura again!

This classic form "Kismet" is truly one for vocal strength. It is not an easy piece as it sits in ones vocal range way up there with the gods, but it is a powerful lovely piece of music that can demonstrate real vocal prowess. This is a sultry piece; it alludes to a sex appeal by the tone of the vocal range.

~

Another Hundred People (Company)

This is a great belter song, from the musical "Company" with drama, passion and cynicism. From the Sondheim opus it obviously takes a certain skill. It has a great lyrical line, true drive and shows off real vocal range while demonstrating how to sell a song without selling. As every song is a one act play this is a true story about life in the big apple. It has real drive and passion.

~

I Get a Kick Out of You (Anything Goes)

One of the greatest torch songs ever!!!

Everyone you can imagine has recorded it from Fitzgerald to Sinatra. It works for a man or a woman. It shows sadness, optimism and belated joy all at once. It has terrific syncopated Latin rhythms and is a true love song.

Yet with satire and emotional honesty this song can pack a punch. Cole Porter knew how to write a sophisticated lyric and melody. This isn't heard every day and as a result makes a great audition piece.

16 of the Best Broadway Musical Small Parts

- ☆ *Fontine "Les Miserables"*
- ☆ *GIGI "Miss Saigon"*
- ☆ *Charlotte "A Little Night Music"*
- ☆ *Petra "A Little Night Music"*
- ☆ *Freddy Einsford Hill "My Fair Lady"*
- ☆ *The gangsters of "Kiss Me Kate"*
- ☆ *Mordred "Camelot"*
- ☆ *Luther Billis "South Pacific"*
- ☆ *Will Parker "Oklahoma"*
- ☆ *Miss Mazzeppa, Electra and Tessie Turra "Gypsy"*
- ☆ *Alfred P Doolittle "My Fair Lady"*
- ☆ *Yente the Matchmaker "Fiddler on the Roof"*
- ☆ *Vera Charles "Mame"*
- ☆ *Mother Abbess "The Sound of Music")*
- ☆ *Aunt Nettie "Carousel"*
- ☆ *Abigail Adams "1776"*

Fontine

"Les Miserable" has such sweep and emotional power that almost any part is a great one to take. Yet one of the best for a woman is the heart breaking role of Fontine the person who would sell her teeth and hair to save her child, only to die and not be able to help.

Her character is instantly understood and being able to sing one of the great pieces of music of the play and then die is worth doing. "I Dreamed a Dream "is a beautiful song of yearning and disappointment and depravity.

A piece of humor associated with this role goes to Patti Lupone who originated this in London. As most know the musical goes on for well over three hours. Fontine is dead and gone by thirty minutes or so into the piece. Evidently Patti fell asleep somewhere and they couldn't find her for her ending scene where the dead come back to sing their final bars. She wrote of this in her book. Such is the danger of having a long lapse from being on stage but this sure is a part to be off for.

~

GIGI Miss Saigon

When you get to sing one great song "Movie in My Mind" and be banished from the rest of the play that is not so terrible. The sadness of the desperation of the girls who are forced into prostitution in Saigon during the war is truly heart wrenching. The character is almost faceless and anonymous yet the song sung is so dramatic and powerful that if you had nothing else to do all evening this would be a great role to take. A truly great one scene part.

~

Charlotte "A Little Night Music"

Recalling the first time seeing "A Little Night Music", you watch 2/3 of the entire first act pass before an entrance of a new character, and what a part to enter with. The part is filled with wicked retorts and one liners. It must be wonderful fun to play. It is a terrific secondary role in a complicated farce but has true comic weight, a great song to sing and really allows an actress to shine in a part that has not too much to do but adds impact to the overall story.

The character is a wife who knows her husband is having an affair then becomes his device to interfere in someone else's marriage. Her scenes are sharp, witty and acidic with hurt beneath the surface, but truly funny and wonderful.

~

Petra (A Little Night Music)

This is another small part with one of the great Sondheim songs. This is part of a pert fresh wicked portrayal of a woman who is a free spirit and knows no boundaries. She is sexually promiscuous and it is vividly portrayed. As with many parts in "A little Night Music" it is the secondary roles that make up the additional fun and this is one part that is truly worth having fun with.

~

Freddy Einsford Hill "My Fair Lady"

Two scenes or so, and a great famous song that is one the audience waits for. This isn't so terrible a part either. It's almost a throw away role, he doesn't do all of that much, you probably don't even have to act very much but what a great song to sing. The audience will applaud like crazy!!!! The actor here gets a show stopping moment.

~

The gangsters of "Kiss Me Kate"

They march around the stage a lot following the lead and they have a great song to sing that Cole Porter wrote with all kinds of nasty puns about Shakespeare. It is pure vaudeville. Talk about a fun time!!! In fact the lines they have could probably be written in about three sentences but the song is one that has tons of encores because it is so terrific. A great part(s) because you get to sing "Brush Up Your Shakespeare" with all of it's' encores.

~

Mordred Camelot

OOOOH to be so evil and bring down a kingdom!

The part is not that well written but neither is the play for that matter, yet there is a fun song to sing "The Seven Deadly Virtues" and the scenes he plays are yummy nasty little bits. If you have to be in "Camelot" that is a pity in itself, but this part is at least fun even if on stage very little.

~

Luther Billis

Well you might prefer Lt. Cable or Emile as they do have better songs to sing, but for a fun comic turn in "South Pacific" there is nothing wrong with this role at all.

You get to dress up and wear coconuts as boobs in the song "Honey Bun" not to mention that you get some fun comic moments. If you aren't a great singer and have a chance this is a lot of fun!

~

Will Parker (Oklahoma!)

This is more fun than Curly in my opinion. You have the fun scenes and sing two songs. One of the songs is a great one; 'Kansas City". It is a fun role, and terrific second lead part. It has a great amount of comic antics to deliver (picture a male dumb blonde) and Will is the part to play.

~

Miss Mazzeppa, Electra and Tessie Turra

These are second act strippers in "Gypsy" who have maybe two scenes, but they have one of the best songs in a musical that has ever been written—"You Gotta Have a Gimmick". Three faded strippers teaching a newbie how it's done is one of the best moments in the entire show. The lyrics are fantastic ("Once I was a schleppa, now I'm Miss Mazeppa") and the antics that go on during the number always bring the house down. If you can't get a big role, chomp on the bit to get one of these three.

~

Alfred P Doolittle

There is a lot that goes on in "My Fair Lady" and Higgins is the big male lead obviously, but Eliza's father has two fantastic songs and is off the stage for most of the evening. It is the sort of supporting role that is tons of fun and requires great comic timing for creating the character and delivers two musical numbers that have tons of punch.

One of them is "I'm Getting Married in the Morning" and the other is "With A Little Bit of Luck", both show stoppers in their own rights. The thing about "My Fair Lady "is that it is so familiar that to do this part you have to create something special and make it your own.

~

Yente, the matchmaker

Well the part doesn't sing much, but the one liners and the Impact of the character on the proceedings is certainly worth playing this role. In a way this is some of the comic relief in "Fiddler on the Roof". In case you are unaware let me also remind you that the part was originally created by Bea Arthur and is there anyone who has ever heard the recording that can't quote her famous lines in the song '"Tradition".

~

Vera Charles "Mame"

Another part ironically created by Bea Arthur, the witchy side kick of Mame Dennis, the drunken actress friend.

She has two great songs one a satirical one in an "operetta" the other a great classic "Bosom Buddies" that has the most wonderful bitchy lyrics maybe ever written, "If I kept my hair natural like yours I'd be bald". It can't be beat.

This is a great, fun, second tier part to play, one that has great audience appeal wit and charm.

~

Mother Abbess "The Sound of Music"

Rodgers and Hammerstein created maternal characters with great anthems. In "The Sound of Music" getting to sing one of the most famous anthems they ever wrote is a pretty amazing small part. The scenes are not too many, but to be able to Sing 'Climb Every Mountain" is worth doing for the sheer power of the piece.

~

Aunt Nettie "Carousel"

Here is another maternal role that Rodgers and Hammerstein created. The wisdom she is supposed to have is also presented musically with the wonderful and powerful "You'll Never Walk Alone". Although Aunt Nettie is a side player in the story this is one of those parts where a mature woman can really leave a powerful impact, reach the rafters and bring people to tears.

~

Abigail Adams (1776)

There are only two women's parts in "1776" but the part of Abigail has two wonderful songs to sing. It is special and the many letters and imaginary scenes with John Adams make for terrific singing and character building in small space. It isn't a larger part due in part that the actions are about what was happening in Philadelphia. Since there are so few female roles in this piece this could be a gem.

28 Biggest Musical Game Changers

- ☆ *Showboat*
- ☆ *Oklahoma*
- ☆ *Lady in the dark*
- ☆ *Pal Joey*
- ☆ *Carousel*
- ☆ *South Pacific*
- ☆ *Kiss Me Kate*
- ☆ *Guys and Dolls*
- ☆ *My Fair Lady*
- ☆ *West Side Story*
- ☆ *Fiddler on the Roof*
- ☆ *Cabaret*
- ☆ *Company*
- ☆ *Follies*
- ☆ *A Little Night Music*
- ☆ *A Chorus Line*
- ☆ *Sweeney Todd*
- ☆ *La Cage Aux Folles*
- ☆ *Sunday In the Park*
- ☆ *Cats*
- ☆ *Phantom*
- ☆ *Les Miserables*
- ☆ *Miss Saigon*
- ☆ *The Producers*
- ☆ *Hairspray*
- ☆ *Next to Normal*
- ☆ *Fun Home*
- ☆ *Hamilton*

Showboat

As mentioned earlier, Edna Ferbers' sprawling novel seemed to be an unlikely candidate for a musical. It has a 50 year span of time, had an integrated cast which was not a normal occurrence, ran for three hours plus. These were not normal situations for a Broadway musical in its era.

Hammerstein and Kern knew that they were looking at

something very unique and Ziegfeld also noting the value of what was to be written wanted in as well and he produced it.

This time period's musicals were often referred to as Princess musicals where an ingénue would be engaged and the comic antics of the engagement and ultimate wedding were the frequent plot mechanics. There was tap dancing, songs that were not connected to the plot, placed for audience enjoyment not meaningful plot development.

'Showboat" was different in that the characters were constructed with real issues. The impact of gambling addiction on a family, and the issue of race were at the core of the "Showboat" story.

"Showboat" today remains one of the only musicals of the era that we would consider. Its score is magnificent and familiar. It is operatic in scope and sadly requires an enormous cast. At the time Showboat was an enormous hit and set the stage for the evolution of the modern musical. It was ahead of its time on many ways.

~

Lady in the Dark

It is still considered a major game changer of the time. As noted earlier it is an important musical of the era, and in the development of the modern art form. Looking at it today we would have to wonder what all of the shouting was about.

The story of a woman having an affair and trying to decide who she should shack up with seems a bit trite. She is so shaken up by her behavior that it would send her into psychoanalysis, in creaky 1940ish ways, but frankly the style of the piece, how musical numbers were interpolated into dream sequences during sessions with her analyst was inventive and truly unusual.

The use of turn tables to create the story was a very big break through and the Kurt Weill music was uniquely sophisticated.

Although rarely seen today this was a major advance in character building and plot devices to music.

~

Pal Joey

So ahead of its time it was hidden away for another 11 years after its debut as it was considered way too racy and lewd for popular audiences. The idea of a leading man without any likable characteristics seems not so unusual by todays' standards but in 1940 this seemed odd and out of sync with popular entertainment attitudes.

"Pal Joey" was sophisticated entertainment, sexy in its approach and considered by the morals of the day very R-rated. The lyrics of the songs were so "racy" they had to be augmented so that they could be played on the radio. One of its most famous songs "Bewitched Bothered and Bewildered" had several verses changed so it could be recorded.

Was it really that racy? No, it isn't at all by today's standards but a man being kept by a significantly older woman was pretty adult and the story telling was not the typical musical of the time.

Today this musical is rarely seen as the book is dated in approach. Yet in 1952-3 Jule Styne resurrected it for a significant Broadway run. The ideas presented were a bit more tolerable and audiences were accepting more mature themes.

~

Oklahoma!

As discussed earlier, this is considered the water shed moment for the modern Broadway musical.

The Theatre Guild had approached Richard Rodgers who was having a terrible time with his partner Lorenz (Larry Hart) a sadly depressed alcoholic... Hart said that turning the play "Green Grow the Lilacs" did not reflect his vision of sophisticated urbane lyrics and did not want to do it. Once this became clear the Theatre Guild approached Oscar Hammerstein who clearly was almost a washed up lyricist/ librettist at the time. His style of writing seemed passé and not what current tastes were looking for.

As the team developed their strategy they wanted a play with music, they did not want a chorus of girls opening the show and instead created deep characters that used dialogue that was written before the sings to convey who they were.

The opening, after the overture, was a male voice offstage singing A Capella, a woman churning butter on her porch and that was the beginning.

The characters were all young at a time when maturation and coming of age was their focus. On the surface Oklahoma is a simple story about a girl who wants to go to a picnic. Yet below the surface is the story of complications of sexual desire and awakening.

The evil character in the piece is a mysteriously dark man who may have raped or murdered. It is unclear. A loner, he collects pornography. The secondary female lead sings a telling song "I Caint Say No". Then there is the story of the travelling salesman Ali Hakam. All of the characters seem to have a sexual longing.

Yet the most revolutionary section of the musical was of course the "Out of My Dreams" ballet. You see the entire story of "Oklahoma" told in a dream ballet sequence which ends the first act. It was bold. THis style of ballet was yearned for in musical but never achieved before.

There is also the new style of love song they created where the characters do not profess their love exactly in a romantic fashion. They used conversation. "People Will Say Were in Love" truly is a conversation between two people not the traditional love duet.

There are even the earliest hints of a theme that they explored further, racism and class struggle. There is a song that truly tells you that—"The Farmer and the Cowman?" read the lyrics listen to the song. It is clear there is a class struggle going on.

Oklahoma changed everything about the musical, becoming the longest running of the Rodgers and Hammerstein musicals.

~

Carousel

The famous play "Liliom" had been frequently discussed as material for a treatment to music. Puccini had even wanted to create an opera of the play, but Molnar the author refused. Molnar was taken to see "Oklahoma" and decided that the team of Rodgers and Hammerstein were perfect to create the treatment to "Liliom" that so many had hoped for.

The locale of course was shifted to New England. Classism, the neuveau-riche and those left behind was a true message of the play. The sins of the father being passed onto the child haunt the second act and of course there is redemption, with an upbeat ending.

Here too the ballet is used to highlight the story. The opening did not have a traditional overture; it had "The Carousel Waltz", introducing the characters bit by bit through dance sequence. In the second act there is the ballet Billy sees from heaven portraying his daughter's misery as she is scorned because of his earlier actions.

A further development in style was to give Billy an eight minute soliloquy upon learning that he is to become a father. This had never been done in a musical before.

There is also sexual tension. This love story needed a new way to present the characters feelings. There is the new invention of the 12 minute bench scene, as it is called, where the song 'If I loved you" is sung. This is called a suppositional love song, as it asks the question, not "Do I Love You" rather "If I loved you?"

We are used to hearing it sung straight through but in reality it is a series of shorter sections, interspersed with dialogue.

Carousel was a great follow up piece to" Oklahoma" and in many ways, may be their best work.

~

South Pacific

Yes much has been said here about "South Pacific". How could it not be considered ground breaking? In 1949 this was a very contemporary story about the war, a very recent remembrance for so many that the musical was truly topical and poignant.

This blending of the stories from the Pulitzer Prize winning "Tales Of the South Pacific" by Michener was set into motion by focusing on several key characters. This initial thought process was to take the story of Lt. Cable and make that the centerpiece. The story ultimately centered on the love story about Nellie Forbush and Emile, which added the layer the team needed to create a success.

Immediately, the team knew the play was going to have

the subtext of racism. It was a complicated topic and the ideas of using ballet to tell part of the story was quickly dismissed. The fear they were creating a modern "Madam Butterfly" also concerned them.

There were many challenges to the mounting of the musical, mostly about how the audiences would react to the subject matter that was just beneath the surface. The producers concerns about the song "Carefully Taught" and the battles with the creative team to eject it were enormous. Audience alienation was the fear. Rodgers and Hammerstein were adamant in their belief that the song stayed or the musical had no value and would close the show. They of course prevailed and this was the key to "South Pacific" winning the Pulitzer Prize.

Over time this has become not just a great one but to me among the greatest.

~

Kiss Me Kate

Cole Porter, in 1947, had not had a recent success. His frivolous style of musical was quickly fading. Realizing that tastes were changing and knowing that integrated music and story had not been his usual style he looked at the use of "Taming of The Shrew". Turning it into a musical was brilliant. He wrote the words and music and deeply connected them to the script. The result was his longest running hit He quipped that he could do by himself what took Rodgers and Hammerstein two to accomplish.

This was also the first Tony Award winner for a best Musical as the Tony Awards had just been established.

When one looks at clever banter vocally and in dialogue in two contexts it is brilliant stage craft. A play within a play was novel. The style had not been tried before or after as successfully. Shakespeare became a re-invention in two musicals but "Kiss Me Kate" took the genre to new examination as a source for a musical entertainment.

In 2015 the album was added to the Library of Congress national recording registry as "cultural, artistic and/or historical significance to American society and the nation's audio legacy".

~

Guys and Dolls

Frank Loesser had become a successful song writer and had already had a success on Broadway. The musical based upon the stories of Damon Runyon with characters who never had been seen before on Broadway. These characters were astounding.

From the made up streets in the made up Times Square the characters did not talk like real people but rather the imaginary types that inhabited this stylized New York. In its day it was considered quite brilliant and due to Abe Burrows troubles with the House Un-American Activities Committee the Pulitzer Prize it had been awarded was withdrawn.

This is one of the great masterpieces of the American Musical theatre.

~

My Fair Lady

Many had considered creating a musical of the great Shaw play Pygmalion. There was no traditional love story, no place for chorus numbers and the social issues in British society seemed impossible to express...

Imagine, they originally wanted Mary Martin to play Eliza and she turned it down (thankfully). The musical used the 1938 movie of "Pygmalion" as a jumping off point and further elaborated on certain sequences and off stage events to be added to the musical.

The musical was written in competition with MGM who also wanted to have it created. Lerner and Loewe went after the project by writing it on "spec, winning the backing they required because it was a better than what MGM wanted to do with it.

Many scholars consider it "the perfect Musical". It captured everyone's attention at the time. It is a beloved li production and movie. It would be hard to imagine that there are people who have never seen "My Fair Lady", but in today's world of musical theatre aficionados that is entirely possible. If you know someone who has never seen it, get them to.

~

West Side Story

Reviews at the time were not overly favorable to the musical. It seemed dark and horribly violent. Not everyone was a fan of the Bernstein score. Many thought it was most hyper active and blaring.

"West Side Story" changed everything about how musicals would be portrayed. It didn't end with a happy ending which paved the way for "Fiddler" and" Cabaret". It was truly an ensemble piece, although there were 4 lead characters only one of the four is a truly well-constructed role. It is a unique piece where the music and the choreography are the stars. It re-set the tone of what a musical could become yet was truly to become one of the great Broadway musicals.

The characters are rather flat. Because this is an ensemble piece driven by the Jerome Robbins Choreography it creates a different sort of blended narrative. Yes of course there is a script, but the leads are the mechanics of the story and the story becomes more vivid as the leads are caught in the star crossed story. Truly the way the story gets told using dance as an active component changed Broadway.

~

Fiddler On The Roof

It is a truly universal story about how a younger generation challenges their parents. It is not a new story, as this was even obvious in "Bye Bye Birdie" and "The Flower Drum Song". Yet setting a story in a world where deep hatred because of anti-Semitism existed, and then tracing the breakdown of traditional community thoughts and wisdom somehow connected universally to audiences.

"Fiddler" was conceived based upon the stories of Shalom Aleichem, but the stories, as they were written, were not really much help to the construction of the musical. They became a jumping off point and were craftily re-written by Joseph Stein. They stories became far more accessible and far more poignant than the originals as a result.

"Fiddlers" creators believed they were creating a truly ethnic musical with little wide spread appeal. They knew there was a segment of the world that would flock to it, yet did not imagine as it was being written that it would become a story that was truly universally accessible. The story of generational challenge and their traditions was universal, far more so than initially realized and the sad endings of both acts demonstrated new story telling techniques for musical theatre. "Fiddler" although it has its cartoonish portrayal of the Tsarist era village at times, with deep emotion and honesty packs a punch because of the deeply honest and believable story with in. This was a true theatrical milestone and outran the big musical entertainments of the day to become the longest running musical in the era.

~

Cabaret

Isherwoods' "Berlin Stories" had already created a play "I Am A Camera".

With Hal Prince at the helm, with Joe Masteroffs' book and the Kander and Ebb score took the written page of a Broadway musical to new heights. The great thing about "Cabaret" which was not understood so fully at the time was that its sense of style, presenting the evils of society had far greater dramatic potential then many realized.

Creating an evil character that only comments on, but does not participate in the story, representing society in Germany at the time, was a different approach. Having a love story with a bi-sexual character and a female lead character that has an abortion were not normal character traits in a musical either. Think back to "Pal Joey" and see how some advanced sexual ideas played out and it is a marvel at how far the musical had come by the mid 1960's. "Cabaret" is a musical with great symbolism and depth showing societal decay.

The musical was envisioned to be startling and the huge mirror that was to be part of the original set, allowing the audience to see their reactions, the all-girl band and the rise of Nazism as a text of the musical were not average run off the mill entertainment devices. The characters all seemed truly grounded in the traditional sense of musical storytelling. Yet the darkness and the deep commentary by the MC character all lead a sense of foreboding.

"Cabaret" set the musical options into a new level of storytelling. All does not have to be light and happy.

~

Company

Time and place are amazing for new works. They can rise or fall based upon cultural attitudes at the time. Sondheim taking the George Furth "one act Skits" about marriage, setting them in New York circa 1970 (present day then but period now) highlighted the cultural changes in relationships that were emerging. In the midst of the sexual revolution this was cutting edge. This was still the era when certain expectations were that you went to a musical and came out singing the music you may have just heard. Changing styles allowed music as a vehicle for character expression, not to sell a hit song to be recorded for the radio.

The new evolution of the musical was that a concept or idea could be expressed without a plot line arc as tradition had held. A "plotless "musical could be created and achieve vibrant success because of the brilliance of the words and music that gave the characters life.

This was the first of the collaborations that would occur between Hal Prince and Stephen Sondheim. It still has a great relevance to it and to some the music and lyrics are still better than the book, but it is a milestone.

Follies

A picture of Gloria Swanson in the rubble of the Roxy theatre spawned a musical. The ideas of having former show girls attend the reunion and realize their dashed dreams and hopes could have a musical that would be a success. In its original we all know that "Follies" was not a great resounding success.

It was expensive to produce, the book did not seem well written enough to be worthy of a Best Musical Award. Yet the winner that year a rock musical version of Shakespeare's "Two Gentleman of Verona" has faded from view and "Follies" has become a cult masterpiece.

The score, capturing moods of another era, has become the repertoire of many a cabaret singer. The original cast recording was butchered by RCA and the needed two record recording was not created. It took 14 years to have a recording, as a fundraising gala, which ultimately gave "Follies" its great recognition. As a concert it was able to feature the top, top people of the era, Carol Burnett, Barbara Cook, Elaine Stritch, Lee Remick, Mandy Patinkin, George Hearn, and Comden and Greene among the cast. It is the defining of a great classic.

The musical is glorious and among the best Sondheim ever wrote. The production however requires a size that even today is way too expensive to deliver easily. Yet "Follies" is and was a game changer as well, another plotless musical where the characters revealed who they were in song far more creatively than had ever occurred to date.

~

A Little Night Music

This is a favorite. At least in my top 5! It is a perfectly constructed piece of musical theatre. Great characters! Lush wonderful music, intelligent storytelling and above all it was different.

This was the era of rock musicals that were not doing any justice to anything, and the era of revivals that were rehashing old war horses. Book Musicals weren't working at this point in time. Yet, Hugh Wheeler created a terrific book and of course the Sondheim score features his most famous song "Send in the Clowns"

The story goes that once Stephen Sondheim took on the Bergman film "Smiles of a Summer Night" thinking of it as a waltz musical someone challenged him that he couldn't write it all in ¾ time. Of course he could and wrote an entire musical in waltz tempo variations. The trios, the quintets and the entire choral motifs that were created are not like any other musical before or since. In some ways the opening 'Night Waltz" is a derivative of the "Carousel Waltz" some thirty years earlier.

Why is it among the best?

It showed once again the Sondheim versatility. He tackled anything and created something new and different. It is a special frothy lovely piece. For the truly curious there is a mediocre movie with perfect casting, Elizabeth Taylor as Desiree, and many of the original cast, plus Diana Rigg as Charlotte. Hal Prince who directed it lost interest midway through evidently and the movie is a mess, but if you have the desire to laugh out of frustration, as to how a great piece could be ruined on film this could be it. There was too much potential here to have the results that came from it. This is another example of how Hollywood killed a genre.

~

A Chorus Line

This too was discussed earlier, but has to be included here as well.

It is hard to imagine now that this was so groundbreaking, and hard to imagine that it wasn't. It is almost a victim of its own breakthroughs. Yet in 1975 a plotless musical about the goings on at an audition based upon the true stories of Broadway "Gypsies "was truly a major breakthrough, harshly real and truly shocking. This was genre bending and to this day survives as a catalyst of Broadway musical change. The topics that could be in a musical truly were advanced.

The frankness of sexual issues, the language, the sacrifices of the dancers for their craft were told with zeal and gusto and emotional honesty. For the first time in a Broadway musical a gay actor could be openly and honestly gay, a dancer could talk about buying the perfect body with Tits and Ass, not to mention the long monologue about the young boy who was abused in a porno theatre. All of this plus the honesty about the symbolism of how we are all on the line every day was powerful.

Sadly one looks at it today and it almost becomes a museum piece as it was so groundbreaking and shocking that now it does not shock or surprise. It just plays as a beloved piece of theatre.

The way it came about is still considered controversial as the creators may have taken advantage without giving full disclosure to those who shared their stories. Yet as the New York Times often proclaimed this was a "42nd Street" for a new generation. It was.

It won the well-deserved Pulitzer. It is wonderful, we love it.

~

Sweeney Todd

This is really controversial. It's a love it or hate it sort of thing. It is a masterpiece.

Stephen Sondheim wanted to write a musical that would enrapture the audience while at the same time scare them to death. The musical based upon a play by Christopher Bond seems an unlikely target for a musical but with the Sondheim skill attached it certainly created a lot of excitement. Of course as with most Sondheim works it was not universally accepted as a great masterpiece at the time, yet ever since 1979 is has developed its own audience of respect and is a cherished work. People were frankly horrified at the subject matter. It is Cannibalism as terror.

Sondheim has said much about this in post the 9/11 era. It is even more relevant how revenge and one person's vengeance can impact a society. With school shootings and other horribly violent occurrences that have plagued us in recent years this is not such a stretch to comprehend. The musical has been widely accepted by Opera Houses as a new piece of repertoire and the success of so many productions truly makes this the masterpiece that it is.

Never before had Broadway seen anything like it and if you look at the mega musicals of the British era that followed suit this was a precursor. This piece when done with the proper approach is really fantastic. The score is so complex that to hear the original Tunick Orchestrations, one still marvels.

Then to hear the incredible lyrics that tell the tale!

This is a piece that upon examination created new heights. In many ways, not realized by the creative team at the time, this led the way for the big British musicals to come.

La Cage Aux Folles

Jerry Herman musicals were not successful during the 1970's and the idea of taking the French play" LA Cage Aux Folles" and turning it into a musical was certainly risky. It is truly an old fashioned musical with a central love story although a unique one for the time. Two gay men being at the center of the piece was a new territory.

You may even wonder why this was one such a big deal. The reality is that this had never been done before and the risk of having a gay love story was truly on the edge of insanity. How would the suburban audiences react? Would, there be heavy handed messages?

It made the relationship legitimate and it also for lack of a better word introduced the theatre crowd to accepting the couple without compromise. It was risqué, emotional frothy and yet considering the writer, fairly low key. The Harvey Fierstein book did not hammer gay rights at anybody but certainly drove the issues home that couples come in all shapes sizes and forms. It was a first. It may have been sidelined for years after its original run due to the AIDS crisis, but time has been kind to the piece. It has aged well

~

Sunday In the Park With George

When you can take a famous painting by a painter you know very little about and create a musical with a made up back story around it that is groundbreaking. This was Sondheim after Hal Prince. James Lapine and Sondheim created new territory as well, and to think that a musical about a painting could have punch! This too was a new form of storytelling, There are no real chorus numbers, the characters often comment on their social issues and at its; heart is a very small story ab out detachment and connection.

The dots that the painter uses truly are a detachment of sorts and thus the character embodies the art by being detached himself. The beauty, of course, in all Sondheim works, is the themes that each character owns musically. In this one George the painter sings staccato until he connects the dots in his own life and then sings legato phrases. It is masterful writing. Some say it is really a one act musical that is incredible with a second act that is not so great. Really? It is a musical that asks us to think about the costs of being an artist.

It too won the Pulitzer Prize which solidifies its place in Musical theatre History.

~

Cats

Well many thought this a big boring event, many loved it to pieces and it ran on Broadway for years with the logo 'Cats, Now and Forever" everywhere you went in Manhattan. You cannot ignore the financial impact this musical had on marketing musicals.

As discussed earlier, it was based upon the poetry of TS Eliot and produced by Cameron Macintosh.

"Cats" was a phenomenon; it changed everything about how one markets a Broadway Musical. Yes it had the required Television ad, and yes it had the regular ads in papers but merchandise for sale with the eyes of the cat on it anywhere became the new standard for getting revenue for the show.

"Cats" is the last musical in recent times to have a hit single song that was played everywhere from the score of the musical. The song "Memory" became a well-known pop song and there has not been another song since that reached its' popularity that had its roots in a musical. The Eliot estate was clear that all of the poems had to be used in the creation of the musical. The musical was totally sung and the actors all took on the persona of real cats through movement costume and makeup. This led to the future Disney concept that the show is the brand not the actors in it.

As a plotless musical it kept the style of the "concept" musical alive. The plot was about choosing a cat to have "a jellical life" and all of the cats in the community present their tales to the audience. It also utilized a very unique staging idea where audience members could sit on the stage. This was a "happening" and most audiences truly loved it.

The junk yard was the entire set for the musical and the use of hydraulic lifts was dramatic staging. "Cats" love it or hate it is a Broadway Milestone. It is now the third longest running musical of all times. It was a great show to take the kids to see and many loved it and saw it over and over because there are so many cat pet lovers. You can't hate "Cats" totally. It is too unique but it isn't the most exciting musical around story wise and to some it is a yawn.

~

Phantom of the Opera

This is another you either love it or hate it musical. Certainly the tenure on Broadway is fairly amazing. It has been playing for a generation if you consider the 25 years it has been running. A horror version of the classic tale" Beauty and the Beast" was enthralling as it opened because of the pop and operatic like score that Andrew Lloyd Weber created.

The Scope of the production as created by Hal Prince gave it a lush beautiful presence. His ingenuity made it look as if "thousands" were on stage. The masquerade sequence is full of mannequin figures that move and sway as if they are real.

When it first appeared it was among the biggest of the mega musicals of the time. It achieved instant popularity and acclaim, even though the reviews weren't truly that wonderful. Crossing the Atlantic it had a built in acclaim based upon the London popularity. This musical also began the controversy of having British actors transfer to do their parts here when American actors could have taken the roles.

One can't argue with the popularity the piece has achieved over its' lifetime. Touring around the world multiple times certainly has built its following and in the it's early years was the production to see. It is a highly successful commercial piece of theatre, it cannot be argued. Going to the theatre in this era and not seeing it is a terrible shame. It is a solid entertainment. A beautifully crafted piece of theatre and one can still admire even now 27 years after its debut.

~

"Les Miserables"

Another of the big British imports of the 1980's that sheer size of the production alone made its mark. It too made its mark. The story, so universally known, with its pop opera score was emotionally vibrant to thousands of theatre goers for a very long time as well.

The score still lush as ever and the enormous production was a tremendous crowd pleaser. Many compared this often to the "Phantom of the Opera", but why go there? Both had their merits, and candidly "Lez Miz" is my favorite of the two.

The scale of the production was a new ilk for Broadway at the time and the lavish use of hydraulics and set turntables made the sprawling story even bigger. The libretto, though not totally faithful to the epic novel that is its' source created stirring passions, and emotions through its "pop-opera" presentation. The characters, although not always fully developed in song become tragic, real and full of raw emotion.

To this day this is still the real granddaddy of the style of the time. It stirs reactions, creates beautiful images and is pure magic.

~

Miss Saigon

Taking an opera that is well known and making a pop opera of it commenting on the Viet Nam era is still enthralling. Consistent with the style of the time, it too was bigger than big. Its' famous helicopter evacuation scene as Saigon falls is legendary and the cast was as large and populous as Southeast Asia itself.

Yet it was a truly small story surrounded by all of the bigness. It packs a punch and of the biggies at the time maybe the most realistic. This story really happened over and over. It is a reality that we face today, a generation later, the remnants of the Viet Nam war.

This also too ran in the new model that Disney exploits. Once the big names left no names were needed for the run as it became the phenomenon to see because of its sheer size. You did not need stars as the musical itself was the star. This is also the last successful British import of the era. The times changed as did the ability to mount a production this large. Yet for the scope of the production the beauty of the story telling this too is a must see musical of the era.

~

The Producers

Zany and crazy! The new millennium created musicals that were for the first time in years American. It was of course the story of a 1950's era down and out producer trying to make more money from a flop than he would have from a hit. The ensuing gags, borscht belt humor and antics were the genre. The reviews created a mega hit that was the record setting winner for Tony Awards. This musical was of course purposefully tasteless, and not for the chaste or prim! No one could pass being offended. It was satirical, outrageous and made mega stars out of Nathan Lane and Matthew Broderick.

After the original cast departed the producers of the hit capitalized in Disney fashion on the brand not the stars and ultimately may have made a marketing mistake. Great comic pairs might have kept the show running forever much like "Chicago", but that was not the strategy. Further a, milestone of sorts, the arrogance of the production team. They decided that this was such a hit the close up rows of the theatre would be $450 per ticket. That was a first for a Broadway musical that was later copied by others. It was felt there were people desperate enough to pay that outrageous sum to see the show and sit up close.

"The Producers" also solidified the continued trend that many Broadway musicals would need to be based upon existing movies to succeed.

~

Next to Normal

Very sophisticated ideas were now being told to music. The story of a family and the impact of Mental illness on everyone involved do not seem to be musical theatre at all. Yet the story of this family achieved Pulitzer Prize recognition because of its daring serious nature. The "New York Times" said of it at the time" that it is not a feel good musical, but rather a feel everything musical". That was a truly an appropriate and valuable description of the piece. It was numbing to watch and the seriousness of the story told to music, even with the humor it had was difficult to watch without being totally worn out at its end.

The tragic consequences of a family coping with long ago issues that were never faced startled audiences. The long slow decline of the family and its' impact is both compelling and contemporary. It addresses how people hide in their fears and often never recover.

Audiences muse all of the time that you don't leave a theatre singing any longer. That may be true. Musicals today are about creative story telling that propels characters. It is not about selling hit records.

~

Book Of Mormon

If we had not had "The Producers" we never could have had "Book Of Mormon". It took satire and raunchy humor in a new musical to a new level. The story lampooning organized religion among other crazy issues was so tasteless and in your face that had the story not had a warm heart the message would not have worked. What makes this work is at the core it is a real feel good musical.

It used the "truths" about "Latter Day Saints" and stretched them to the boundaries of logic. The focus on two young men, who by church custom, go on their mission in the world to convert uses that as a coming of age story. That is not so unusual. Instead it is a vehicle to create satire. The story is similar of many we have seen before, yet because of its' unique posturing, with its sharp comic jabs it is a musical for a much younger generation. The language is of the times, nothing is sacred and it is not for the faint of heart, prim and proper.

It certainly is really raunchy, but this is a new way to demonstrate what is acceptable as entertainment in a musical and it really works. This will be a long running hit of our time and what we will recall in the new musical era. Exploiting the Disney approach no stars are truly needed as the brand itself is the musical. People flock to it as it is the musical itself that people go to see, not a famous name.

~

Fun Home

To be clear, this very difficult musical to watch stretches the audience. It is bold, it is different and it is groundbreaking. The story of a family that is living with deep lies, and how it impacts the relationships they have. It is brutal yet sensitively told. The story of a young woman, who comes out to her father as a Lesbian only to learn that he has been a closeted, gay man, is complicated emotionally. Add in how she reconciles her father's suicide is truly horrendous to watch. She has lived with the guilt that she added to his death as he could not face his own reality. It is a gut wrenching saga beautifully portrayed.

The father is an unpleasant character who is presented with few redeeming characteristics. It is true he loves his family but he is so troubled by his life choices that his impossible disposition is in itself horrendous to watch. Your heartaches for the family, and to make it worse this is a true story. No anguish is spared on any level. The story telling to music is certainly outstanding, yet it is not easy going. The dramatic impact of how these characters, in true book musical fashion tells their story is remarkable. Yet to be truly honest groundbreaking as it is for the way the story is told, it's not what one would say is universally enjoyable.

This furthers the trend for a musical with a small cast to pack a punch. It follows the direction that "Next to Normal" set forward. It also follows the psychological impact of family challenges. It is hard to say if this is what is called an enjoyable evening of theatre. However it is the boldness of the story telling that makes this so powerful.

~

Hamilton

As the NY Times said, in the first sentence of its review, "yes it really is that good".

On paper none of this would make any sense. A rap/ hip hop score, totally sung, telling the story of Alexander Hamilton, based upon a lengthy biography featuring ethnic actors as the founding fathers.

However musical theater scholars are gathering around to share that this is so groundbreaking that they cannot believe how exceptional it is.

Skeptically having seen it in its last preview week, it was stunning to see a story about our history being told with such fervor, stunning creativity, excitement and power. Who really knew anything about this founding father? That in itself is the magic of the story. Here to a new sound of music the accurate story of how our nation's leaders fought and survived is quite a tale.

It isn't one component that makes it work, but rather an entire mixture of style, presence and storytelling combined. It may be too early to tell but this will be the landmark musical of our time.

19 Great Women's Musical Parts

- ☆ *Mama Rose (Gypsy)*
- ☆ *Fanny Brice (Funny Girl)*
- ☆ *Eliza Doolittle (My Fair Lady)*
- ☆ *Anita (West Side Story)*
- ☆ *Dolly Levi (Hello Dolly)*
- ☆ *Sally Bowles (Cabaret)*
- ☆ *Nellie Forbush (South Pacific)*
- ☆ *Mame (Mame)*
- ☆ *Mrs Lovett (Sweeney Todd)*
- ☆ *Dot (Sunday in the Park With George)*
- ☆ *Fosca (Passion)*
- ☆ *Diana (Next to Normal)*
- ☆ *Carrie Pipperidge (Carousel)*
- ☆ *Mrs. Anna (The King and I)*
- ☆ *Phyllis and Sally (Follies)*
- ☆ *Roxy Hart (Chicago) and Velma Kelly (Chicago)*
- ☆ *Charity (Sweet Charity)*
- ☆ *Lola (Damn Yankees)*
- ☆ *Bess (Porgy and Bess)*

Mama Rose

The Lady Macbeth of musicals, as many has referred to as the greatest part ever written for a musical. The character who sacrifices her children for her own dreams only to be brought down by the very dreams she had is a terrific work of character, conflict and song. Any actress who has taken on the role has to be prepared to the comparisons she will face but the part is so powerfully written that the show works no matter what. The only thing an actress could do to ruin this is to not be able to sing.

The musical demands are pretty strong especially the final soliloquy 'Rose's Turn" which so aptly names what the character goes through including her breakdown.

This is a hard role to top!

~

Fanny Brice

This is a tough one! It is so deeply rooted in the original creator that to tackle it one has to be very, very brave. Yet it is a terrific part, the rags to riches story with all of the heartbreak one can imagine in a personal life thrown in. A great part, in almost every scene and truly an emotional roller coaster in the music as she grows from comic waif on the Lower East Side with determination to a major star with personal heart break.

It is a hard part to tackle primarily because of the association—you can't change perception and since no one else has truly tackled it the inevitable comparisons linger on.

This is a great part and one day it will become not just the ownership of one person.

~

Eliza Doolittle

What a great role for a soprano who has to allow her range to show itself off the longer into the evening the character plays. The flower girl who gets refined is a very famous part and truly the center of "My Fair Lady".

The musical demands lots of lower register singing early on and as the play continues the register gets higher and higher into a coloratura range. There are comic scenes, scenes of emotional power and strength and the character grows in multidimensional ways emerging as a very strong person. In some ways Eliza creates a very independent role of a strong willed woman fighting for a chance long before the woman's movement got started.

It's a wonderful part to tackle.

~

Anita (West Side story)

The challenge to "West Side Story" is that it is truly an ensemble piece. Most of the parts, as already noted, are not multi-dimensional, yet the part of Anita, the second female lead has the best songs of the women in the show (She sings "America") and has the most believable character. She is fierce, loving and tempestuous.

You understand her rationale for everything that happens throughout the play she adds color and life yet becomes tragic as well. Anita is a far better part then the virginal Maria who is the center of the story.

~

Dolly Levi

Now this would be fun! Yes you need tons of personality, lots of charisma that crosses the footlights and a voice that will enthrall (at least in character fashion). The plot line is slight and the story line really pretty silly but the character that holds it all together of the title is the fun part to play. For an actress of a certain age this would be a real hoot to play. It's a fun light hearted role and above all the lead role in a very famous musical. The comparisons to get beyond would even be a fun challenge as there have been many Dollies. You may not get compared to the original at all. Comic timing is critical and the eating scene in the second act is a tour de force.

All of her motivations are not truly clear and perhaps in the Thornton Wilder version it may be clearer, there are questions about Dolly that are vague. How long was she a widow, how did she become a matchmaker, why did she leave the Harmonia Gardens and what was her role there? This is a benchmark role.

~

Sally Bowles

This is truly not an easy role. The original Sally, as directed by Hal Prince was envisioned not to be a great singer. She was envisioned to be a free spirit who would be destined to be "a never was" (forget being a has been). To be that true free spirit that has no real ties to anything or anyone has to be still empathetic because of her true ignorance. The fact she engages in a love affair with a Bi-sexual character, gets pregnant and has an abortion is central to the character. She has to think naively that she can surmount any issue that comes before her.

She too is a symbolic of the way a culture ignored the future. She ignored her own.

Of course music gives the actress the opportunity to shine, even though it has been taken on by real singers, that is not so critical to the role. After all Judi Dench did it once upon a time and she couldn't sing like Liza! This must be an actress who can sing and show an amoral side to her persona. This too is an ensemble piece with a story that has deep darkness surrounding it. The actress has to take on the part without having a sense of the future or real desperation. That is not an easy task. She has to be someone ambitious enough to be blind to reality, and clever enough to outwit herself continually.

~

Nellie Forbush

This possibly could be the best female character that Rodgers and Hammerstein ever created. The naïve, love struck young woman who is in the midst of a war very far from home, falling in love with a mysterious French planter on an island, much older than she and then to find out he has dark skinned children is a lot of character to tackle.

The music builds the character and thanks to Mary Martins' fear of being overshadowed by Ezio Pinza musically there are no love duets. Instead there is a lush soliloquy, several great character building songs and the anguish of knowing that she may have given up someone she truly loves.

The ideas of racial prejudice provide the deeper angst for the character and should not be seen as trivial or secondary to the motivation. This is a character that sparkles and then has real fear of longing, losing and coping with many out of character issues. She embodies the lyric of "Some Enchanted Evening".

What a great part!

~

Mame

Yes it is a musical entertainment of it's' time, and the character in the original nonmusical version may have been far more fun, but this is a star building role and can be a real scene stealing fun ride. The actress has to have a madcap sense of comic timing, be able to belt to the rafters and then when required have heart breaking yearning.

The musical score is fun and there is comfort that Jerry Herman wrote great musical moments for the character to sing. There are great musical moments. How wonderful to sing "If He Walked Into My Life". What's wonderful about Mame is she is always stylish, ahead of her game, and way ahead of her time. It's a wonderful story and sweetly even tugs at the heart strings.

The final sequences are not as satirically clever as the original to give her enough to do to prevent a bad marriage for her nephew, but still the character is a marvel.

~

Mrs. Lovett

Having once been in" Sweeney Todd" it is something to reflect back on the work it takes to pull off Mrs. Lovett, the evil catalyst of the treacherous revenge story that is the basis of the musical. The ability to be comic, appear witless but sly as a fox, and sing the incomparable lyrics Sondheim has created to his fantastic music is not an easy task. The character has to for a large part of the evening seem sympathetic, or at least likable until it is time to realize she is the devil incarnate and has created the monster that Sweeney Todd has become. She fanned the flames and is herself the embodiment of the injustices of the era.

What makes this work is the comedy that lies beneath the surface of this very dark tale. This may be the best role in musical theatre after Mama Rose. It might be one of the most difficult and challenging. In most musicals you play the part and deliver what is written for you. Yet in this one the complicated music and lyrics add another dimension to the expectations. The true Sondheim fans know the piece and that is not easy to get over. They know what to expect and wait for it to be delivered.

Imagine singing while pounding dough!

This is one masterful part to play and is an incredible challenge at the same time.

~

Dot (Sunday in the park)

The center of a painting that becomes the central female candidate in a love story that has an emotional blank as a counterpart is not an easy character to portray. It is a terrific part, the actress even gets to play a ninety year old version somewhat of herself in the second act. The musical challenges are obvious as Sondheim created lots of intense and vital music. There is frustration to portray in the first act and true warmth and sincerity to portray in the second act. In many ways the second act character is directly out of Rodgers and Hammerstein as the wisdom of age is what is presented to the character of George.

Dot, clearly is the supporting role to the male character but even so must have a strong character of her own to sing her guts out for.

~

Fosca (Passion)

Talk about a complex complicated role. The audience may clearly hate you! You even have to look ugly which is a challenge. Sondheim wrote this part for a great contralto with lush passionate vocal singing. The character has to evoke complicated emotions and desire while being totally shunned. She also has to not appear to be a stalker, rather someone who has deep desire for someone she knows she will never have for her own.

It's not an easy part to portray as it is mostly an unsympathetic portrayal yet at the same time this is the most romantic musical Sondheim ever wrote. Fosca is a challenge to take on and the rewards of doing this can be truly masterful.

She has lush lyrics, and the depth of the vocal range is truly haunting in its construction. In addition the character must somehow find a way to get the audience to understand that there is something there to love and that is not so easy with a person who does everything she can to embarrass, stalk and inhibit someone she loves from afar.

How the actress can create compassion is central to the success of the portrayal. If done well it is mesmerizing.

~

Diana (Next to Normal)

The devastating effects of depression and bipolar disorder in a family are heart wrenching. The lead character in this stunning portrayal must be able to be empathetic, sympathetic and brilliantly sung with gut wrenching heartache. The musical is not an easy one in fact it is almost unbearable to watch. The story of a family being destroyed by the weight of mental illness is a heavy role to endure.

To tackle this requires a skill and depth that separated an actress from the pack. The pop rock score, the emotion in the ballads, the anguish are very heavy to take on. This may be among the most challenging roles for a Broadway Musical actress. It is wonderful rewarding and exhausting.

It also shows what the modern musical theatre is creating roles for its divas to create.

~

Carrie Pipperidge (Carousel)

Yes this is the supporting female character but a lot more fun to play than Julie Jordan who mopes around and has to be so whiny, proud and somewhat unsympathetic for her choices. Rodgers and Hammerstein created musicals with secondary female leads and this one has the comic songs that are beautiful and far more fun to sing. "When I Marry Mister Snow "is a gem. Carousel" can be so emotional and it is a tear jerker. Yet the comic relief here is by far the most enjoyable part in the entire musical.

~

Mrs. Anna (The King and I)

The part written for the great Gertrude Lawrence is among the great parts written by Rodgers and Hammerstein. It is almost a feminist feast written before that even became fashionable. Mrs. Anna is a head strong character who takes on a king, becomes his counsel (at least in the story) and then seemingly through interference in his affairs breaks his will. Who cares that this is all fabrication.

However, she educates both herself and the children she was hired to teach. This is a play about classism, and racism in the mode that the team had begun to explore in earlier works. The idea that Siam was a lesser place in the views of the English is clear. Further you have another very strong female character who, ahead of her time took charge of her own destiny.

There is also the impact (subtle as it is) on Women's rights both in the character of the Kings first wife, Mrs. Anna, and Tuptim. Mrs. Anna becomes the catalyst of many story nuances and devices and in many ways may be among the best drawn characters in the Rodgers and Hammerstein opus.

It is a great part and to wear that great big dress in "Shall We Dance" must be worth everything. The role is comic, sensitive, wise and courageous. The music written is among the most famous of the Rodgers and Hammerstein creative works and certainly a joy for any soprano to sing.

~

Phyllis and Sally in Follies

Take your pick. One part is frumpy and dumpy and the other is sleek stylish and bitchy. Both are scenery chewing in their own way as the music Sondheim created for these two women is nothing short of incredible.

Phyllis of course is the Upper East Side matron who "stole" Sally's man way back when and the two duke it out at the reunion they are attending.

Sally is the disillusioned, emotionally disturbed housewife from Phoenix who can't let go of her past. The script, at times, has been accused of being nothing more than one liners, but the music the women sing is gut wrenching, passionate, and of course gloriously Sondheim. This score is among his best over written. The women get to sing some of his best! The anguish of singing "In Buddy's Eyes" a delusional song of lies the character tells, or "Could I Leave You" the bitter anguish of woman who knows her husband has never really been focused on her is another masterpiece.

To pick one part over the other is a hard choice.

Sally Sings the great torch song "Losing My Mind" and Phyllis sings the fantastic "Story of Lucy and Jesse". They are both wow songs and not to mention what comes earlier is pretty fantastic as well.

~

Roxy Hart (Chicago) and Velma Kelly

These two female leads in "Chicago" make the entire production. One is "cupey" doll fun, dumber than a sly fox and truly conniving. The other is a real sly witch. Of course this is a dancer's show not to mention a belter's delight.

Velma and Roxie are cunning murderess and the two vie for recognition in the crazy media driven frenzy over murder trails. Were it not based upon reality and the OJ Simpson or Nancy Grace era we might have a harder time accepting these characters.

The Kander and Ebb score is fantastic, the book terrific and of course to be a part of musical theatre history by portraying two great characters is fantastic.

Velma may in fact have a better song to sing (All That Jazz) and she is in the 'Cell Block Tango" .Yet as the tossed over woman by the attorney they both need is still a great part to play. She has the bitter wit throughout most of the evening and has the amoral 'Class" to sing with the matron.

Like in "Follies "take your pick and have a feast of fun portraying two great female parts.

~

Charity (Sweet Charity)

The only problem with this is that Neil Simon did not create a well written part. In fact it is not great comic stuff. The character makes little sense. This is about a woman who wants to be loved. As was typical of Neil Simon his musical characters did not fare well as he did not write the lyrics they sang and there was a disconnect between the way the character sang and the way they talked.

Charity was problematic as she truly should have been written as something other than a taxi dancer (whatever that is).Yet the part is a tour de force, and the for a dancing Broadway personality you could not go wrong performing such an exuberant role. The musical numbers are terrific and all said and done it's a good show, even if not a perfect one. This is one of the great parts to play in musical theater.

~

Lola (Damn Yankees)

It's not the biggest part of all time that is for sure, but what fun to be the Devils' chief home wrecker in "Damn Yankees". It is a sexy, sly, wonderful fun plum role. It is not lead status really, but it is a big part and the music that they give the character great music to sing and dance to. The classic stuff of Broadway legend is what the part is made up of. You just can't go wrong with this if you are a sexy siren type who can dance their legs off.

~

Bess (Porgy and Bess)

Talk about the courage to take this on.

This may be the greatest role for an African American woman ever written. The musical requirements are staggering and the stamina substantial. To be able to sing the greatest score ever written as Sondheim says something to the effect"that there is Porgy and Bess and then there is everything else".

The operatic natures of the part are truly challenging, the character she must create, make this a critical role for any African American actress. Even though she is deeply troubled and could be seen as not sympathetic, this is a true character. Even though Stephen Sondheim in his famous letter to the NY times about the recent revival bashed Audra MacDonald for tackling this watered down version, it is a masterpiece and a role that should be tackled.

The challenge besides the musical demands is that Bess must create empathy and understanding of why Porgy loves her, yet at the same time must convince you that she can't help herself. At some level she loves Porgy as well, which might be hard to comprehend due to his physical challenges. The audience has to see the passion they have.

20 Great Musical Parts for Men

- *Billy Bigelow (Carousel)*
- *Tevye (Fiddler on the Roof)*
- *Porgy (Porgy and Bess)*
- *Nathan Detroit and Sky Masterton (Guys and Dolls)*
- *Sweeney Todd (Sweeney Todd)*
- *Cervantes (The Man Of La Mancha)*
- *The MC (Cabaret)*
- *J Pierpont finch (How to Succeed)*
- *Jean Val Jean (Les MIsearbles)*
- *Javert (Les MIsearbles)*
- *George Seurat (Sunday In The Park With George)*
- *Albin (La Cage Aux Folles)*
- *The guys in the producers (Max Bialystok and Leo Blum)*
- *Psuedelous (Forum)*
- *Edna Turnblatt (Hairspray)*
- *Alexander Hamilton (Hamilton)*
- *Henry Higgins (My Fair Lady)*
- *The Devil (Damn Yankees)*

Billy Bigelow (Carousel)

This is a part with wonderful character, full of passion and drama and great vocal moments. When "Carousel" was being written they created a part where the character is seriously flawed, not good at communicating, not well educated (obviously) yet wanting to love and be loved. He uses his best asset, his looks and charm to be his fortune. He does not know how to handle that, and his emotions are so driven and out of control that he even hits his wife.

When he discovers he is going to be a father, a masterful compelling 8 minute musical soliloquy (a musical theatre first) gets to be sung, then uses bad judgment and dies shortly thereafter. He then gets to see earth from heaven and try to right the wrongs he left behind. Now if that isn't meaty!

This is a baritone role that is a character worth doing the stamina of the "Soliloquy" is nothing but ferocious. It also gives a baritone the ability to really sing some of the greatest music Rodgers and Hammerstein wrote for a male character.

You also have a terrific opportunity to learn the "Bench Scene" which is a 12 minute scene with dialogue that includes "If I Loved You".

~

Tevye

Taking away all of the pre conceived notions that come with this part, it is one terrific role. Recently I saw a Tevye that was not a caricature of the way many have seen the role performed before and truly emphasized the world crashing down around him as changes were forced upon him. It was different and not the caricature the role can become if played too broadly.

Yes there is a very distinct ethnicity that comes with this role, and yes there are expectations but that does not limit the actor form creating a sympathetic father who is forced to re-examine everything he has believed. He loves his children and his faith and it is that balance that becomes the forceful dynamic.

If you think about it, Tevye is not as old as many think he may be in reality. Being married 25 years he could have been

18 at his wedding. This would put him in his young 40's. This is important as Tevye, in the time might not have been much older than that and it also has to be imagined that Tzeitel his oldest is not much less in age either than 20. Very old for an unmarried woman in those days, she too may have been a late blooming teenager!

This can be a wonderfully nuanced portrayal walking away from the unprofessional approach that eventually inhabited Zero Mostel who broke character all of the time and did his own thing with the part nightly. He was not the cherished favorite in the role as he continued to unprofessionally murder it.

It is a truly emotional sensitive character that has deep beliefs and makes this the part that it is. Think of "If I Were a Rich Man", not as a cliché but as a passionate dream soliloquy and it takes on a different meaning. So many moments make Tevye a tragic comic character, yet he is not tragic to himself which is the beauty. He has hope due to his faith. That becomes the magic of the part.

~

Porgy

For an African American this would be the part of the century. This is the quintessential character, lovable, naïve, needy and of course madly in love with someone that will never really be his. Add in the profound and dynamic Gershwin score and powerful strong singing that is a requirement of the role and you have a power house of a part. This is a masterpiece of a part, one that requires strong singing, acting and presence to show the hurt and optimism that the character possesses. He has a childlike naiveté in his love for Bess. His passion is a strong powerful emotion that carries the entire folk opera.

When he leaves for New York to tragically go off and find Bess he too is doomed because of his naiveté. To portray a character that has unlimited optimism and can never really win would be powerful to accomplish.

~

Nathan Detroit or Sky Masterton

"Guys and Dolls" has two great parts for men, not to mention the supporting players that surround them. To choose one over the other is almost odd because both a perfectly written characters that send exuberance and thrill into the audience. Sky is the more singing role of the musical and Nathan the more comic role but both are real gems.

The wonderful thing about "Guys and Dolls" Is that the dialogue is written in a certain style that works with real comic appeal, yet you see real characters being developed who grow and change (comically).

The music that Frank Loesser wrote for these two characters, although Sky sings much more, is truly wonderful and great stuff for a baritone to share with an audience. These are parts to go after; they certainly did not hurt Nathan Lane or Peter Gallagher in 1992.

~

Sweeney Todd

This is one of the greatest.

In the 1840's, a man who was sent to prison in Australia on trumped up charges comes back to London. He steals away to search for and to find his wife who some years ago was stolen from him by a wicked judge. The bottom line he is seeking vengeance! This is a juggernaut of a role. It has deep passionate complexities.

The part is so much to sing, and with such power that Len Cariou developed serious vocal damage from the role. The music requires anger, fierce energy, and humor and must show a tortured soul to be at least empathized with as he creates terror everywhere he goes. To be able to truly be the actor who can justify murdering people to get even with society for punishing him and then baking them into meat pies must have some sort of empathy and compassion. He has to be believable and watchable at a level. This isn't easy to portray and Sweeney at the same time has to be understood as to why the neurotic results occurs to make this watchable.

The musical piece "Epiphany" is such a powerful combination of music and drama that learning this one alone is worth the part.

There is a great deal of energy in the role, but the terrorizing energy that the performer must muster, creating a sympathetic side to the terror. It makes this an incredible part to take on.

~

Cervantes (Man of La Mancha)

Sometimes parts become caricatures of themselves because at the time they were preformed they were seen one way and after that they are seen another. Cervantes is an odd character because he must play the author awaiting his certain death from the inquisition and at the same time portray the character Don Quixote who searches for love and wisdom everywhere. He is obviously a bit mad. The characters in the jail cell with him take on the persona of those in his tale of a man chasing windmills and this actor must be strong enough to not become a cartoon himself.

Another challenge is that everyone sits and waits for 'The Impossible Dream". The audience does wait for the moment to swoon. The song is not even that difficult to perform but it can't be over performed and over amped . The result is it becomes a cliché very quickly. This is one of those pieces that touch memories because of the era it was created in. IT can sink a performer who over emotes all of the way through it. The presentation has to be humble and naive yet demonstrate great foresight and wisdom at the same time.

This can be a wonderful part for a Baritone and if the tried and true expectations of the role can be bypassed with a unique characterization up so the actor is not in a portrait of a part; this is a wonderful one to play

~

The MC (Cabaret)

This is another one that could be tricky. It has two very different famous portrayals, one created by Joel Gray and the other created by Alan Cummings. Both represent evil and the character is not truly the main actor of the musical. In fact the actor in this role may not have any real lines as his scenes may be all sung or close to it. Yet the character is the moving influence that shapes the arc of the musical by being a Greek Chorus of sort to the actions on stage. He must be so far out of the societal norms that he himself is the surrogate of the evil of the regime to follow.

It is a stylish part that knows no specific boundaries and interpretations as it has been successfully reimagined from the original. The role can become as grotesque and creative as an actor could envision.

The musical numbers are a great pastiche of commentary and are truly what gives the musical its extra punch.

~

J Pierpont Finch (How to Succeed)

This is a favorite part to watch, it too is tricky as it can't be seen as too devious or smarmy. Finch has to be truly lovable. If the satire is remote he is a pretty cunning guy. It often is portrayed by young (alleged) innocents. Think Matthew Broderick or recently Daniel Radcliffe. The part doesn't really need that but it is the history of the role. The cuter he is and more "Nebbishy" the better. The character could be seen as a total snake, but has to be charming, sly like a fox and lovable.

It is a fun role to play because it is a satire and not a serious moment in the play is ever taken too seriously. Yet the part had great moments, great music to sing and truly a fun role to inhabit.

~

Jean Val Jean

Ahhhh, for the tenor in us all who loves "A" flats this is the best you can attain. It is a warm large and wonderful role. Jean Val Jean has to loom large and feel the pain he feels always feeling insecure all the while by being a solid rock.

"Les Miz" is an emotional experience for all who watch it and to be Jean Val Jean, the center of the story is a powerful task. The recent turn of casting seems to be that actors of any age can portray this man as it is the warmth of the character that enables a good actor to own this role. In fact currently actors of color are taking on the part which certainly is within the realm of the story form a contemporary vantage point.

Of course the totally sung part, with much of the onstage time being his is no small task.

~

Javert

If you are a Baritone and Jean Val Jean is not your idea of a match then this is the part to go after. It has real juice to it and had great vocal moments. Being the bad guy (or one among several) is a fun place to play. There are wonderful vocal moments and to be the catalyst that propels the story is a wonderful part to play.

"Stars" is a terrific piece to sing and the suicide scene is great singing and great drama.

~

George Seurat

The idea that a character who is a pointillist sings staccato until he connects his own dots has always intrigued me. Sondheim gave beautiful characterization musically to a persona that is within the total consistency of the plotline, and what the character develops. It is two different people in two different acts, 100 years apart, but the musical themes that run through the performance are consistent for both characters.

The vocal range and to be able to deliver with punch "Finishing the Hat" is no small feat musically. It is a part that truly requires masterful delivery. The actor has to have a remoteness that is charismatic and must determine how to seem isolated deeply involved in his art and yet connected. He himself represents a dot as he is not connected to anyone. That too is symbolic of the character and the bridge between pointillism. It is a brilliant conceit.

~

Albin (La Cage Aux Folles)

This is a great part. Playing a drag queen that has to deal with mid-life challenges, then identify himself to be ok with who he is in the incredible anthem "I Am What I am" is a masterpiece of character delivery.

The ability to play a character in drag, and to be truly believable at it as well as touching and not a caricature is a difficult feat. Yet this part is so "round" and robust that it is the better of the two parts in the musical to play. You use his fear, his desire to be loved and his insecurity at not being so. Many actors have played it and each differently There is a charisma that has to be evident and prominent, but the character does not have to bluster and can be portrayed in a truly multi-facetted style that is not predetermined.

This is a ground breaking role and was way ahead of its time.

This is one of those parts that would be killer to play!

~

The guys in the producers Max Bialystock Leo Bloom

Max or Leo take your pick. These are two great comic parts, each with their own shtick to sing and carry on with. Max of course is the coarser more conniving part pf the two, and Leo the weaker sniveling yet equally sly buddy role here.

Max is the epitome of sleaze; he chases old women for their money, lies cheats and steals all the way around. Yet, and he too has a heart in there somewhere beneath the Borscht Belt Humor. Leo on the other hand is a guy looking for a life of meaning and value. He hates his dull mundane existence and as this is all satire fights to get out. He is equally as sleazy as the plot unfurls.

These guys are the satire of Broadway, sort of left over from "Guys and Dolls" if Mr. Brooks does not object to the character comparison. They are not real; certainly they are cartoonish but fully dimensional people in their own satirical ways. These are tour de force comic roles and take vigorous energy yet must have a likable dimension or they fall flat.

~

Psuedelous (Forum)

For a person that really has terrific comic timing, doesn't really sing as their major talent, but can handle the Sondheim score this is a surefire winning role. Once upon a time it was even portrayed by Whoopie Goldberg, so the part is unisex of sorts, and it works because of the frenetic pace the character plows through. It is not serious stuff on any level but anyone who has taken the part and uses lunacy to add to their portrayal goes over the top as a winner.

It is a great part, not a one man show, as this in many ways is an ensemble piece. It allows for great comic mastery. A truly fun antic role that is truly ageless for the actor that takes it on, it is almost any size, shape, or type that can take it on and win!

The opening number alone is more fun than anything to

sing. It's such a famous opener that to sing it and be the event of the evening in and of itself would be terrific. The actor gets to over act and emote like crazy, be sly and silly and above all carry on like a lunatic and get away with it.

~

Edna Turnblatt

What a woman on the man part list, of course.

Yes that is correct as the conceit of this part has always been that it is a man in drag (a very large man or one in a fat suit) playing a woman. It works as there is a deep sincerity at the core of the role and even though that part is comic, and even cartoonish, it has the basis at its core of telling a story, loving womanhood in all sizes and shapes and discovering respect for oneself.

The actor in this role may not have the best songs in this play but the role itself is the center of the play, even though the part could be considered the secondary lead. It's really about how she sees the world and changes because of what she allowed herself to endure. The actor has to somehow convey outside of the cartoon requirements that there is a role here of reality.

It is not a caricature; it is a solid part with depth and dimension. It looks like a cartoon, but it isn't at all. This is a real woman under those wigs and oversized costumes, just being played by a man. If one doubts the reality of the conceit, in the 1600's Juliet was played by a man don't forget!

~

Alexander Hamilton

Maybe it's too new to say so, but this part written by a genius Lin-Manuel Miranda who saw the possibility in writing a musical about the life of Alexander Hamilton would be a masterful accomplishment. None of the rationale makes sense on paper but seeing it live it is a part to tackle. It may never be played by a white man ever as that is the conceit of the way this structured. Yet to take this on, another ageless part really you have to be able to do the rap and hip hop score that the part requires. It is totally (or almost totally sung) which requires tremendous strength and capability)

This part over time will be championed as the part that may have reinvented the lead of a musical, or what a lead must be able to accomplish. It was amazing to see what takes place.

Hamilton has faults, serious flaws and visible drive and ambition. Yet he was a founding father of our country which also has us question how we even were able to pull this off.

~

Henry Higgins

Maybe the best role ever written for a musical, the stubborn irascible dialect coach who is too class egocentric to ever really fall in love with anyone but himself is a part of great dimension. He has to be totally aloof, caring and maniacal and become likable to the audience while being a temperamental, self-absorbed egotist.

The great mastery of the part is to establish the classism that the role requires. This is not an easy feat! He himself snubs the British expectations of certain manners, yet he picks and chooses to set his own important class choices .The snobbery of the English class system has to be evident and it also has to be deeply respected and thought about for the aloofness to have a charisma and warmth.

The musical ability to not sing a role but be a person who can get the music to the audience is a style that they wrote for Rex Harrison. Doing it any other way than the way it is usually heard puts an actor in dangerous territory. The actor has to do it to the style we are accustomed, somewhat sadly. Having seen the role performed sung rather than "spoken sung" it was truly off putting. It is now a convention of the role.

It also is an ageless part of sorts. Henry Higgins may not have to be ages older than Eliza and that may be the fun of the approach. It would be fun perhaps to see a younger actor play Higgins who really feels jealous angst over Freddy Einsford Hill.

~

The Devil in Damn Yankees

It is not the lead and in fact a supporting player to the story who is the catalyst, yet this has to be more fun to play than many roles.

The actor gets to be snarly, mean spirited and lovable all at the same time. You can imagine signing your soul over to him!

It is a character part of sorts, could be played by almost anyone with great comic timing and he has one really great song to deliver in the second act, 'The Good Old days". It's a delicious one scene stealing little song but a fun one. It's a fun character part; he has tantrums get so act in infantile manners and is just plain ridiculous fin. It could be an actor of any age.

It's not the biggest part ever written for a male actor but this is really a fun one.

57 Great Musicals With a Backdrop in Show Business

Before we get to the list, it is a huge list, we will mention many musicals that were based upon a show business background and not even try to discuss each one. It is a huge and lengthy list. It is interesting to ponder how interesting that backdrop is to storytelling in a musical. It is hard to discuss each one but suffice it to say that if the list is examined every one of these has a plot device or back drop with a show business story. It is an interesting situation to consider as to why so many musicals use this as a backdrop.

- ☆ *42nd Street*
- ☆ *Kiss Me Kate*
- ☆ *A Chorus Line*
- ☆ *Annie Get Your Gun*
- ☆ *Applause*
- ☆ *Showboat*
- ☆ *DOREME*
- ☆ *Bye Bye Birdie*
- ☆ *Jersey Boys*
- ☆ *Funny Girl*
- ☆ *Spamalot*
- ☆ *The Boy From OZ*
- ☆ *Gypsy*
- ☆ *La cage Aux Folles*
- ☆ *Carnival*
- ☆ *Million Dollar Quarter*
- ☆ *Me and Juliet*
- ☆ *Memphis*
- ☆ *The Producers*
- ☆ *Curtains*
- ☆ *Nine*
- ☆ *The Drowsy chaperone*
- ☆ *Dreamgirls*
- ☆ *Follies*

- ☆ *Barnum*
- ☆ *Cabaret*
- ☆ *Ain't Misbehavin'*
- ☆ *Sunset Boulevard*
- ☆ *George M!*
- ☆ *Beautiful*
- ☆ *Chicago*
- ☆ *On the Twentieth Century*
- ☆ *Phantom Of the Opera*
- ☆ *A Little Night Music*
- ☆ *The Full Monty*
- ☆ *Kiss Of the Spider Woman*
- ☆ *Babes in Arms*
- ☆ *Anything Goes*
- ☆ *Sister Act*
- ☆ *Mack and Mabel*
- ☆ *City Of Angles*
- ☆ *Chaplin*
- ☆ *My Favorite Year*
- ☆ *Can-Can*
- ☆ *Singin' In the Rain*
- ☆ *Guys and Dolls*
- ☆ *White Christmas*
- ☆ *Victor Victoria*
- ☆ *Pal Joey*
- ☆ *Sound of Music*
- ☆ *Bullets Over Broadway*
- ☆ *Side Show*
- ☆ *Crazy For You*
- ☆ *An American in Paris*
- ☆ *Something Rotten*

25 of the Most Interesting Musicals Based Upon Movies

Rather than debate the merits of each of these, and to not be redundant here is a list just for the list sake. Much of this material has already been covered elsewhere here so reiterating it again would not add any real additional insight.

This is just another way to look at a fascinating Broadway List.

- ☆ *The Producers*
- ☆ *Hairspray*
- ☆ *Sunset Blvd*
- ☆ *La Cage Aux Folles*
- ☆ *The Full Monty*
- ☆ *42nd street*
- ☆ *Nine*
- ☆ *Wonderful town*
- ☆ *Sweet Charity*
- ☆ *Little Shop Of Horrors*
- ☆ *Wicked*
- ☆ *Grand Hotel*
- ☆ *Sunset Boulevard*
- ☆ *Light in the Piazza*
- ☆ *Grey Gardens*
- ☆ *Spamalot*
- ☆ *Billy Elliot*
- ☆ *Kinky Boots*
- ☆ *Promises Promises*
- ☆ *Once*
- ☆ *Phantom of the Opera*
- ☆ *Passion*
- ☆ *A Little Night Music*
- ☆ *The King and I*
- ☆ *An American in Paris*

My 10 Favorite Broadway Musicals

People ask me all of the time what are your favorites. So to put a list out there for all to see here you have it,

MY Top 10 Favorite Broadway Musicals (not in any particular order)

- ☆ *Sweeney Todd*
- ☆ *Gypsy*
- ☆ *Follies*
- ☆ *A Little Night Music*
- ☆ *Hamilton*
- ☆ *South Pacific*
- ☆ *Chicago*
- ☆ *Fiddler On the Roof*
- ☆ *Les Miserables*
- ☆ *Cabaret*

Blown Away

First of all I hope you are having imaginary discussions and even disagreements with me (even if we haven't met) about your views of the musicals included on the lists. It's fun harmless argument.

I keep thinking about the lists I didn't tackle (at least yet)

The 15 best Broadway Leading Men

The 15 Worst Casting Choices

The 20 Best Musicals Set in NYC

The 15 Best Leading Ladies

The 5 Best Sondheim Musicals

The 5 Best Musicals David Merrick Produced

The Best Musicals of the Great Impresarios

10 Musicals That have become overdone clichés

It goes on and on—

Recently I had one of those OMG experiences. While lecturing at sea on well-respected upscale cruise line going transatlantic from Barcelona to Florida all of my reasons for writing and creating this once again came to life.

I have had so many experiences where this material has connected to so many that I was reminded once again on the recent crossing how Broadway Musicals are a personal and popular genre.

The people I have met are the reason I had to do this. For

example the woman that was Rosalind Russell's niece, or the man that danced with Julie Andrews in "The Boyfriend", the sister of the man who wrote "The Drowsy Chaperone", Patti Lupones' 8th Grade English teacher, Richard Rodgers next door neighbor, Alan Menkens' first cousin, and even the woman whose husband was the first violin in the Shubert theater for 35 years. These people shared the side stories of how Broadway Musicals impacted them and how my lectures brought back great memories.

I think of two people I met while lecturing that made me really smile.

The first was a woman that wanted to meet me. I was told she was 103, and played the piano still two hours a day. I had just completed a lecture about the 1940's shared the development of "On The Town" and she wanted me to know she knew Leonard Bernstein at Tanglewood as she was the choral director there. Can you even imagine?

Recently I was giving a lecture where a man came to me and said that he was so thrilled that he loved musicals. He told me that when he grew up in Manhattan if he had 35 cents he would skip school and go to a Wednesday matinee. I asked where he lived in Manhattan, he told me. I then said my dad grew up in that neighborhood. I mentioned my Dad went to a certain high school and he said so did I. Then I mentioned that my dad would at that time have been 96. The man replied I'm 96. He asked me my father's name and sure enough he said I knew him and I almost fell over.

As we hear music on the Broadway channel, we all have our favorites. Even our favorite dislikes. During a recent question and answer session aboard ship someone asked me something really odd. "Why didn't she like the new musicals compared to the old ones". She became specific about the ones she did not like, some of them were truly wonderful, but they were different.

I did not want to insult her taste as she went on to elaborate on her favorite oldies compared to the new works.

It's all perspective.

What makes this so special to me is that so many of us love the genre. There is a thrill to think that 1000 people would come out of the sun at 1130 in the morning on a cruise ship to listen to my perspective about the musicals we love.

I somehow thought about the lyric in "A Chorus Line"— "dance for grandma, dance for grandma why did I pay for all those lessons?" Here I was at my mature age, standing in front of 1000 people talking about my passion, singing selections from the musicals we love and being appreciated for the knowledge and the ability to still credibly sing. Looking at those 1000 people as the mic went on I blurted out "if my parents could see this". All of my singing lessons have paid off.

Tears rolled down my cheeks.

Made in the USA
Lexington, KY
03 July 2016